D1797827

Making the Shift to the Model Church

Making the Shift to the Model Church

THE CHURCH IS IN THE MIDST OF A MAJOR SHIFT

Bill Vincent

RWG Publishing

Contents

Copyright © 2023 by Bill Vincent

All rights reserved. No part of this book may be reproduced in any manner whatsoever without written permission except in the case of brief quotations embodied in critical articles and reviews.

First Printing, 2023

1

〜

Understanding the Opposition

The Enemy will oppose you if you are feeling God's power and presence at any level. This is a day when identifying the oppositions is key to breaking spiritual strongholds. We are in a period of transformation, and it is imperative that we understand our adversary. The ruthless adversary will want to frustrate us at every point on the transitional ground. That is why the purpose of transitional periods is to deepen our reliance on God. We must learn how to cling to Jesus' majesty and sovereignty. It's all too easy to blame the enemy, blame others, or look for a human justification for our circumstance while we're going through change and transformation.

I believe that God wants to give us a divine rationale because, despite my limited contact with God, I believe that God wants to give us a divine rationale. I've come to realize that God allows what He could easily avert with His power because of His wisdom. We want to know God's wisdom if He is allowing certain occurrences.

16:12 (John) I still have a lot to say to you, but you can't take it right now.

Because of their own perception, He was restricted in what He could do in their hearts and speak into their lives. The Lord is constantly working to improve our understanding of what He is doing. That is what we refer to as a "revelation." Right today, the Church may be said to be like that. The deep is calling out to the deep. I can't remember ever feeling such a weight of Heaven weighing down on what we're doing. Angelic sightings are becoming more common over the planet. Demonic manifestations that are more forceful and unusual are likewise becoming more common. On top of the normal, the supernatural is folding itself layer by layer. Heaven is yearning to visit us here on Earth. There are currently more intercessors on the planet than there have ever been in the Church's history. These days, there is a significant amount of intercession. Someone is praying fervently in every church, no matter how little. Many churches are at a tipping point in their intercession. It is clear that the entire planet is changing. Deep things are happening in the Church, some of which we don't fully comprehend. I believe that some messages will be delivered to the Church via angelic visitation because we will be unable to bear the weight of them. No one will be able to receive the full weight of revelation from the Holy Spirit on their own. I think that angels will appear, just as they did in the Old and New Covenants of the Bible.

Angels are sent to assist mankind in breaking through when they are unable to do so. They function at the locations where Heaven meets Earth, where importance must be transmitted, and where God's designs and purposes must emerge dynamically. They are ministering spirits who have been dispatched to deliver a message or offer assistance at a key juncture. Their numbers are growing on the planet. For churches to achieve that heavenly cutting edge of spiritual gifting and character, this is a genuinely extraordinary period. In a world where rationality is driving people insane, we're breaking new territory and becoming more prophetic. Things are passed via prophetic churches ahead of time. As a result, we will be singled out for criticism. This will undoubtedly benefit our humility. God created human conflict to draw us into grace.

We gain more power as a result of demonic antagonism. All opposition is set up to work in our favor. We shall learn to be generous and merciful in the face of human hostility. We'll learn to love our foes, pray for those who persecute us, and bless those who oppose us. Demonic resistance is meant to teach us how to stand in the Lord Jesus' authority and might. Its purpose is to demonstrate Jesus' majesty and sovereignty, as well as to teach us how to surrender to God.

James 4:7–8 As a result, submit yourself to God. The devil will fly from you if you resist him. God will draw near to you if you draw near to him. Cleanse your hands, you sinners, and your hearts, ye hypocrites.

Every action taken by this form of church is based on advancing truth. Other churches will not understand the emerging Revelation until it is manifested in something visible. This requires perseverance on our part, so that our critics can one day join us in spirit and truth. We must continue to pray for the Lord to open the eyes of our religious saints, so that they may see and comprehend what is unseen and hence beyond their comprehension. To work in the supernatural realm, the church need a complete paradigm shift. We can't hope to defeat the devil by following the laws of reason and reasoning. We can't hear words about the future unless we're willing to change our current habits. We'll see what God sees, say what He says, and do what only He can do simply because He wants us to. To share the Holy Spirit's perceptions, we'll have to suspend our skepticism.

If we are to enter the growing kingdoms of God, we must first recognize, isolate, and defeat the enemy. That is why the prophetic is required. Prophets have a tremendous love for God and a strong dislike for the enemy. They've always been at the vanguard of any fight against lies, fraud, injustice, and oppression. Most biblical figures had a strong prophetic component to their life. Many people claimed to be prophets! Yet, in today's churches, prophets and leadership are thought to be incompatible. We have a church that does not understand process or growth, owing to the fact that those who do are not in positions of authority or actual influence. Reason has taken over from revelation. I adore logic. Except when He chooses not to be, I believe God is reasonable. Then there's the matter of revelation. Wisdom words are supposed to offer us with supernatural reasoning that isn't based on human logic or intelligence.

In order to keep up with God's reasoning, the intellect must be regenerated from time to time. Things that make no sense in the natural world will be revealed supernaturally through divine revelation as God communicates at a higher level of faith and thought. Our thoughts haven't yet become His! On this level of supernatural understanding by revelation, real prophetic individuals naturally communicate with God.

True apostles are gifted by the Holy Spirit with the ability to translate prophetic insight into a strategy for church response and growth. As a result, the new Church will be built on a partnership between apostles and prophets who are all dependent on the Lord Jesus Christ.

Only a few people are aware of the process of transforming prophetic potential into reality. It's one thing to get a prophetic message; it's quite another to watch it come true. Many people and churches I know have had major prophetic utterances delivered over them. Whether or whether any conditions are intended or specified in the prophecy itself, any personal prophesy is conditional. Conditional prophecy is concerned with the possibility of fulfillment rather than the certainty of fulfillment. Our response, as well as our ability to align our hearts and lives in living obedience to God's revealed word in the Scriptures, can cause it to be postponed or even canceled. Unconditional prophesy exists, and it pertains to God's entire plan for mankind. It can be tweaked, but it can never be avoided from happening since it is determined by God, not by human response. To walk with God and see that word fulfilled according to the Lord's decision and timing, as well as our preparation and location, we need endurance and patience.

To make our potential a reality, we will need to collaborate with the Holy Spirit. Working through frustration is an important part of transforming our potential into reality. I like folks who are frustrated. They are one of the church's hopes. The majority of people are irritated because they are concerned about something. They do, however, have a special responsibility to the Holy Spirit to put their frustration to good use.

When people mistreat their relationship with the Holy Spirit, the flesh takes advantage of their irritation to foment dissension, struggle, and division. Instead of being a good prophetic utterance, they will become a discordant voice. Frustration exposes our genuine selves and releases a message that can be nasty and destructive, or good and inspiring. We are interfering with the law of cause and effect if we intervene between our frustration and God's purpose. People aren't always careful enough with their thoughts, especially when they're frustrated. The flesh can seize what the Lord wants if we leave our thoughts exposed.

As a precondition for turning frustration into impartation, we must have a real regard for cause and consequence. We reject the possibility of divisiveness by adopting God's plan. God is always the cause, and whatever is released via the Son is the outcome. Frustration is sent to alter us, to make us more like Jesus; this is stage one of cause and effect. When we allow dissatisfaction to drive us to step in and intervene for others, the result is a flow of impartation that empowers and encourages others. That is, after passing the test of selflessness, we arrive at a point of trustworthy servanthood. The second contains all fear, whereas the first contains all love. As a result, the fight is between love and fear. Do we love God enough to let Him carry out His plan, no matter how painful it is for us? Do we care enough about other people to serve and assist them, regardless of how much we want to be right?

Isaac was not the cause of Abraham's prophecy coming true; rather, he was the result. The only person who could bring the prophecy about Abraham to fruition was God Himself.

18:10-19 (Genesis) And he added, "I will assuredly come to thee according to the time of life," adding, "and lo, Sarah, thy wife, shall have a son." Sarah could hear it through the tent door behind him. Now Abraham and Sarah were both elderly and sickly, and Sarah's behavior had changed to that of a woman. As a result, Sarah giggled to herself, asking, "Will I enjoy pleasure once I have become old, my lord becoming old as well?" And the LORD answered to Abraham, "Wherefore did Sarah laugh, thinking, "Shall I certainly carry an elderly child?" Is there anything the LORD can't handle? I will return to thee at the set time, according to the season of life, and Sarah will have a son. Sarah then refuted it, claiming, "I did not laugh because she was terrified." He said, "Nay, but you did laugh." And the men sprang up from their seats and gazed toward Sodom, and Abraham accompanied them on their journey. And the LORD replied to Abraham, "Shall I hide from Abraham what I do?" Because Abraham will undoubtedly become a big and powerful nation, and all the nations of the earth will be blessed in him. Because I know him, he will direct his children and household after him to observe the LORD's way, to do justice and judgment, so that the LORD may bring upon Abraham what he has spoken of.

Part of our dissatisfaction stems from the fact that we can't see how our lives fit into the current situation unless things change. Can we place our desire and hope for importance on God's altar and rely in Him alone to bring it to fruition? It is a true and thorough evaluation of our reasons, desires, and true servanthood spirit. We shall find out here whether we will take the opportunity for our own interests or whether we will lay down our lives for the sake of obedience.

It was a severe test of Abraham's obedience when he was commanded to offer Isaac as a sacrifice.

Genesis 22:8 says: And Abraham said to his son, "My son, God will give himself a lamb for a burnt offering," and they both went.

22:15-18 And the angel of the LORD called Abraham out of heaven a second time, saying, By myself have I sworn, saith the LORD, that in blessing I will bless thee, and in multiplying I will multiply thy seed as the stars of the heaven, and as the sand on the sea shore; and thy seed shall possess the gate of his enemies; and in thy seed shall all the nations of the earth be blest; and in thy seed shall all the nations of

Only by letting go of our own dreams in the service of God can we keep them. That may be one of the frustration lessons we must all learn if we are to be true servants of God. Our fulfillment is due to His promise and goodness, not to our desire to grasp the promise and make it work.

In his life, David had to learn a similar lesson from Saul. King Saul had chased David with all his might in order to prevent his son-in-law from becoming his heir. Saul was at their mercy when he entered the cave where David and his men were hiding to relieve himself. David's allies persuaded him to assassinate Saul, believing that it was God's will. On that day, David learned that the death of Saul was not the reason for his ascending to the kingdom. It was just God's will and strength to carry out His own promise. David was the only one who could jeopardize God's cause. If we are not focused on God's purpose, conflict will inevitably arise. Our virtuous flesh will come up to defend its position, so justifying itself. Our body has an unproductive and harmful effect on God's cause. In our frustration, we must be ready to accomplish God's cause by our obedience. The result of our disappointment is an outpouring of encouragement, prophesy, insight, and blessing. Achieving success necessitates readiness. When we reach a level of readiness, it will be accompanied by a desire to carry out God's will through His Spirit. The beginning of confidence is readiness.

God knows what He's doing, and we'd rather put our faith in His ability to do it than in our own ability to comprehend it. We all know that everything works out in the end. God, who will not reveal His purpose before the event, will do so after we have trusted Him. He does not always speak at first, but He does always speak. We get ready to do His will by submitting to Him, regardless of how we feel. Frustration is either the spark of life that gives life to a new dimension or the letting go of everything we care about. Do not snuff out that spark, but rather appropriately nourish it. The contemporary leadership issue is one of time, motion, and efficiency.

With so many things going on and so many demands on our time, it appears that regulating some situations and people is easier and more effective than facilitating and developing them. It's easier to say no than to say yes. People must realize that, first and foremost, frustration is an inside issue. It will show the individual where and how the Lord wants to alter them. Leaders must assist them in removing detrimental individuals from the population.

139:23, 24 Psalms Search me, O God, and know my heart; test me, and know my thoughts; and see if there is any crooked way in me, and lead me in the road that leads to eternal life.

We must be certain that our dissatisfaction with anything does not manifest itself in anything harmful to others. We are free to pray effectively and stand in the gap for others once we have allowed the Lord to deal with our own hearts.

How we handle our irritation is a key indicator of our commitment to working with the Holy Spirit. Is it possible for Him to have faith in us? Are we devoted to the Holy Spirit's fruit or just His gifts? Are we more concerned with our own ministry than with the building up of the Body? Frustration is a well-designed criterion for determining loyalty and present attitude. It's an honor to be frustrated. It indicates that if we handle it well, if we demonstrate and accomplish what is on God's heart, a new door in the Spirit realm will open for us. That door will close on us if we miss the opportunity and channel our fury into fleshly activity. It may take some time before the Lord has enough faith in us to reopen that door. Frustration is the opportunity to learn and grow. Of course, if we are perpetually frustrated, we will require counseling and potentially liberation from spiritual negativity, pride, contempt, and arrogance. On a regular basis, our flesh will have gotten the better of us, and we have now become a liability. Our frustration is now being monitored by the enemy, not the Holy Spirit, for the aim of causing friction and division rather than growth and progress. God will transform us first and foremost as a result of our frustration, and then He will change others around us. If we surrender to God, frustration will bring everyone and everything into accordance with His plan. Transition is necessary for our revelation to become experience.

There are two things that we absolutely require in this situation. We require a revelation of the true nature of frustration, and we must recognize that transition is the point at which revelation becomes experience for us. Transition is a time of trial and error.

It's the space between promise and fulfillment where we're put to the test to see if we're ready to live in the place God has for us. Adam was promised that he would rule over the earth and have dominion over it. To determine if he could rule over himself, he was placed in the Garden of Eden. The garden served as a transition zone, a smaller area of influence and activity intended to serve as a testing and proving ground for him. He had forgotten about it. We must be truthful to ourselves. How many times have we been dissatisfied? Is there anything positive and noteworthy that happened during those times? We've missed the purpose if we're blaming others.

Three fingers point back at us for every one we point at someone else. Did those moments of irritation result in further impartation, renewed servanthood, or a test that we aced? If not, these tests will be repeated. Testing is a necessary component of the process of transforming our potential into reality. We can identify who are God's true men and women by their actions. They are the ones who have found inner serenity. They have nothing and everything at the same time. They aren't pushing for anything, and they aren't promoting themselves. They are pleased to put their faith in God. He places items in their hands because He has faith in them. Their annoyance has been alleviated. A continual flow of impartation has taken its place. They've evolved into facilitators for others. They are unconcerned about their position in the grand scheme of things. Great servants are constantly in demand. Trustworthiness is a reward in and of itself.

2

⌒

We're on the verge of a breakthrough

When you transition into a prototype church, you will witness some of the most significant breakthroughs you have ever witnessed. Breakthroughs aren't always readily apparent. Many people are unaware of where they came from. Breakthroughs don't start with the discovery of anything new. They go back far further than we think. They begin when we resolve to seek the Lord through extended, fervent prayer along with fasting.

2-4 in Daniel 10 Daniel had been in sorrow for three weeks at the time. I didn't eat any nice bread, didn't put any pork or wine in my mouth, and didn't anoint myself at all for three weeks. I was on the side of the large river, which is Hiddekel, on the fourth and twentieth day of the first month; Daniel 10:12 Then he said to me, Fear not, Daniel; for thy words have been heard from the first day that thou set thy heart to comprehend and to chasten oneself before thy God, and I have come for thy words.

Daniel had no idea about the breakthrough or where it came from until he was told. Breakthroughs happen when we start praying seriously and are noticed after we've finished praying. Daniel remained firm in prayer so that his supplication before the Lord may be fulfilled. If he had given up on prayer, the intercession that had started on the first day might not have been completed to the point of recognition at a later date. Everything that God does is born out of conflict and struggle. The nation was in the midst of fighting while Daniel was praying. Daniel was completely oblivious of the struggle or his role in it. He had no idea how much his consistent praying had helped in the divine struggle.

Wherever Jesus went, he provoked conflict. Demons would scream in anguish as a result of His presence. The interaction between His presence and demonic forces resulted in healing and deliverance. Some attempted to stone Him, while others attempted to murder Him. If we pray for His presence to arrive, He will bring provocation with Him! We shall join in all of the combat that He instigates.

In times of warfare and confrontation, breakthroughs occur. If you want me to come to give you breakthrough, you should be aware that if you don't have a confrontation while I'm there, you will have one soon after I leave, because breakthrough is inherently confrontational. Breaking through necessitates a fight. To break through, you must be in a war. The opponent must turn against you in order for you to break through. He'll have to come to your aid. You must also go on the attack in order to break through to him.

We will witness a side of God that we have never seen before in times of war. That is why fighting and confrontation are so crucial. We are not scared of it; but, we must learn to like it. That doesn't mean we're all giddy with joy at the prospect of spiritual combat. We can enjoy the struggle once we're in it, but we must first consider the cost. Our God is not scared of anything, and nothing bothers or provokes Him. God knows who He is in Himself, hence He is a God of battle who laughs in the face of His foe. He is completely aware of His own individuality. He desires to imbue the church with all of the features and characteristics of His own battle nature. He only puts them in us on the battlefield, though. So it's time for us to join the war! There are several churches that have still to be built on the battlefield. To be assaulted by the devil, we must be good enough. Most churches aren't equipped to engage in genuine spiritual battle. The enemy does not need to assault them because they are capable of doing so on their own! The devil doesn't need to attack many churches to cause havoc. He can just go in and push a few fleshy buttons: resentment, bitterness, ambition, pride, arrogance, and unteachable behavior. We won't be able to meet on the same battlefield as long as he can hit those buttons. Before we can win the outward struggle, we must first win the internal one. As individuals, we must win the internal war. We must also succeed on a business level, uniting as one people with one heart, one thought, and one voice. Then we'll be ready for serious combat, and all hell will burst out all around us. Then we shall discover that God will reveal Himself in ways we never imagined. When the God of battle appears in the middle of a church, the nature and spiritual capability of that church alters radically!

Luke 22:28-30 You are those who have stayed with me through my temptations. And I establish a kingdom for you, as my Father has established for me, so that you may eat and drink at my table in my kingdom, and sit on thrones ruling over the twelve tribes of Israel.

11:12 (Matthew) And the kingdom of heaven has been subjected to violence from the days of John the Baptist, and the violent have taken it by force.

There is a characteristic of hardship and endurance that births in us a stronger anointing to work God's tasks in times of struggle and warfare. God genuinely believes in us because of the sorrow He sees in our hearts and lives. We can't construct anything without going through pain. So many leaders are turning their backs on misery. Good leadership understands how to suffer; they understand the need of patience and endurance in standing firm. People are free to leave, but the leaders will not. It is during this period that God realizes He can rely on us. He endows us with something. Any time God has increased the anointing on my life (in the last 22 years), it has happened after a period of intense fight, warfare, criticism, or suffering of some type. We take a step back and understand that it was only through God's mercy that we were able to survive at that time. After then, God's blessing came upon us and increased the anointing.

1:12 (1 Timothy) And I give thanks to Christ Jesus our Lord, who has empowered me, because he has counted me faithful in placing me in the ministry; there is a fidelity there that we are both earning and learning to develop in the Lord's heart. That is a change that each of us will go through. We must comprehend the stages that God will lead us through so that we do not flee when the time comes. In church life, there will be some exciting and critical times when everything is poised on a knife's edge. As He teaches us to walk by faith rather than sight, we will gain insight into God's thoughts. His goodness and mercy will be extended to us as well. At the same time as His mouth disciplines us into simple faith obedience, His heart comforts us in our learning anguish.

1:8 Isaiah Come now, and let us reason together, says the LORD: even if your sins are scarlet, they will be as white as snow; even if they are red as crimson, they will be as wool.

3:5 (Proverbs) Trust in the LORD with all of your heart, and don't put your trust in your own understanding.

The question is whether or not we believe, not whether or not we comprehend. We must ready ourselves to walk with the God of the Unreasonable in the next dimension of church. He will challenge us to do the unthinkable, to take on initiatives that are beyond our comprehension. These undertakings will have prophetic underpinnings. That is why the prophetic talent and ministry in our midst must be nurtured. We won't be able to become a prophetic church without it because we won't be able to conceive what the Lord wants to do in and through us. We shall miss the grandeur of God's larger intentions if we don't have that revelatory rationale to guide and assist us. While He wants to give us the city, we will be attempting to take a neighborhood. When God wants to use us as a spark to take the nation, we'll try to believe God about the bigger picture. We consider our own resources as well as the scope of the task at hand, and we make a sensible, informed assessment of our prospects of succeeding. We shall not even attempt the problem if the circumstances appear to be too vast and wonderful.

13:25-33 is a passage from the book of Numbers. After forty days of searching the land, they returned. And they went to the wilderness of Paran, to Kadesh, and gave word to Moses, Aaron, and all the assembly of the children of Israel; and they brought back word to them, and to all the congregation, and showed them the fruit of the land. They informed him, "We got to the place where you sent us, and it floweth with milk and honey, and this is the fruit of it." Nonetheless, the people who live in the area are strong, and the towns are walled and very large, and we saw the offspring of Anak there. The Amalekites live in the south, while the Hittites, Jebusites, and Amorites live in the highlands, while the Canaanites live by the sea and along Jordan's coast. And Caleb brought the people to a halt in front of Moses, saying, "Let us go up immediately and possess it; because we are fully able to subdue it." But his companions remarked, "We will not be able to go up against the people; they are stronger than we." And they returned to the children of Israel with a bad report of the area that they had examined, saying, "The land through which we have gone to search it is a place that eatth away its inhabitants," and "All the people that we saw in it are men of large size." And there we beheld the giants, the sons of Anak, who came from the giants: and we were as small as grasshoppers in our own eyes, and we were as small as grasshoppers in theirs.

When we move forward with faith in God's capabilities, though, things take on a different hue. We, like Joshua and Caleb, shall submit a report that is full of reverence for God's anointing, even if it costs us our lives.

14:7-9 And they said to the whole congregation of the children of Israel, "The land through which we passed to search it is an incredibly good land." If the LORD is pleased with us, he will bring us into this land and give it to us, a land flowing with milk and honey. Only do not rebel against the LORD, and do not be afraid of the inhabitants of the country; for they are bread for us; their defense has been taken away from them, and the LORD is with us; do not be afraid of them.

Here are a few daring faith declarations:

• Do not be afraid of the inhabitants of the land, for they will be our prey; their protection has been withdrawn, and the Lord is with us!

These individuals did not dispute the veracity of the negative story; giants, walled cities, and a powerful army were all present. Joshua and Caleb, on the other hand, were focused on the Lord and His might. The other spies, on the other hand, did the exact opposite and felt insignificant and powerless as a result. Being a prophetic church implies that we live by every word that God speaks directly into our current situation. We don't live on prior words, but on those that come after them. All of God's actions have a revelatory rationale. He is preparing us for the next phase of life in the Spirit while we are in transition. There is a procedure that must be followed and comprehended. With every change, there is a breakthrough. Many churches fail to make it through the shift. Under the strain, they separate.

The most difficult test in a church's history is transition. In the next round, only the best will be able to claim their inheritance. Beware:

the transition line isn't exactly what we believe it is! We understand the transition period is over long before the following step begins.

3

～

In the book of Revelation, a new church emerges

I finished a six-hour lecture series and never got close to finishing anything God said. In the following few chapters of this book, I'll be providing even more detailed writing. For a variety of reasons, churches are in transition. Some churches are transitioning from exceptional local churches to resource churches.

As more people are empowered and freed, this means a broadening of vision and a new level of impact. Some churches are transforming into apostolic centers, with resident fivefold ministries allowing the church to play a global role in church planting and development. Transition, on the other hand, will simply refer to the process through which many churches embrace their corporate destiny at a much higher level.

Revelation is a stage in the construction of the prototype Church that you must go through. When the Lord wants to take us to a new level, He wants us to have more vision, anointing, and power.

An increase in commitment and character is required. The transformation process always starts with revelation, which is an insight from the Holy Spirit, sometimes through prophetic disclosure. A prophetic word is spoken that inspires and fires new faith in our church's future and overall vision. The prophetic word may bring together prior words and our current vision to move the subject ahead significantly. The impact of revelation is significant. It will force us to reconsider our current situation and future plans. Revelation forces us to evaluate and scrutinize all we've done and are doing now. Revelation goes under our skin, making us enthusiastic about what the future holds for us while simultaneously making us scared about what it all means. Revelation denotes a shift in perspective.

It is a beginning that is preceded by an end, a closure, and a fresh beginning, all of which is surrounded by vulnerability throughout the church. The prophetic message fills us with joy. The vision excites us, yet the change it entails makes us nervous. Teaching has the potential to bring revelation. I've been to various churches where teaching on the new church of the twenty-first century or new church models has sparked a fresh vision in the congregation. The members of such body have been swept up in faith and have a strong desire to create such a church. The lecture has acted as a catalyst for the members to begin discussing and dialoguing about structural changes, fresh vision, and a distinct spiritual culture in a new context.

I've been to churches where folks from all walks of life had nearly identical visions. Moving to a new location, establishing a new project, generating a variety of new church initiatives, or a combination of these actions have been the visions. People had dreams in several areas that continued to build a picture of what God was revealing from one person to another.

The variety of people utilized by the Lord during these events has been fascinating. These folks have vastly diverse emotional make-ups, personalities, and relationships. That fact, in and of itself, lends credence to the event's supernatural nature. Of course, we don't make decisions purely on the basis of our dreams.

We do, however, use them as a springboard for prayer, discussion, and further spiritual growth. We can acknowledge that God has acted sovereignly, and now we must make ourselves available to the Holy Spirit and to one another. Revelation can also occur as a result of apostolic understanding and friendship. Our conversations and relationships with our network friends and congregations frequently have an apostolic/prophetic visionary and directive element to them. We look out for one another and pray for them. In times of strain and struggle, we stand together; in the Kingdom, we work side by side, teaching, imparting, ministering to one another, and wishing the best for one another. All of these things serve as a catalyst for new ideas and insights into vision and destiny. Apostles can analyze events in a church's life and offer practical advice on how to proceed.

We expect revelation to emerge from these interactions, allowing us to move forward with prayerful intent. People's hearts are filled with hope as a result of revelation, which is wonderful and hopefully contagious, but it also causes issues for us in the implementation of a new vision.

We want our people to believe in God and have faith in Him. We want as many people as possible to feel this new sense of expectation and excitement. But we must be careful not to exaggerate it beyond what the Lord has said. In trying to gain support for the new item, leaders frequently go too far and transform expectation into assumption. We'll perform well if we can strike a good mix between exhilarated vision and sober difficulty.

The only moment we are spiritually balanced is when we are fully still. Walking is defined as throwing our weight between one foot and the other while maintaining a feeling of direction. As we walk together in harmony, spiritual balance is the movement of obedience and the distribution of faith between vision and sacrifice. If we are unfamiliar with how the Lord like to work, expectancy might be harmful. Although vision and revelation work together to give us a new feeling of purpose, they can also limit our ability to plan thoughtfully.

Luke 14:28-32 For which of you, if you want to build a skyscraper, does not sit down first and calculate the cost to see if you have enough money to finish it? Lest, after he has laid the foundation but is unable to complete it, others who see it begin to insult him, This man began to construct, but was unable to complete it. Or what king, before going to war with another king, does not sit down first and consider whether he will be able to face him with ten thousand men if he comes against him with twenty thousand? Alternatively, when the other is still a long distance away, he sends an ambassador and requests peace terms.

We can get caught up in the thrill of the moment and adopt a "go for it" mentality, only to be caught off guard when the reverse occurs. Reflection is rendered worthless by hype. Consideration is obliterated by assumption. Faith and caution are not mutually exclusive. Faith is ready to take on the challenge! Caution wants to get things right the first time. "Yes!" says Faith. We're going to make it happen." "This is how we should go about it," Caution advises. Caution adds strategy to faith's energy, ensuring that nothing goes to waste. The key distinction between the two is the rate. Faith wants to get there right now, but caution wants to get there safely! Faith will pay whatever the price is; caution will not pay more than is required. "Let's just pay it as we go," Faith suggests. "Let's budget for it before we start!" cautions Caution. Caution and faith are mutually beneficial. In a war situation, caution, not trust, will provide a peacetime budget. Faith will not be able to overcome challenges if it is not guided by caution. Faith is confident in its ability to run a marathon and is eager to get started. Caution understands how to run a marathon, ensuring that trust never runs out of gas. The union of specific knowledge and confident belief is faith with caution. In this case, knowledge entails an awareness of God's ways as well as a grasp of strategy and momentum. In God, everything has a rhythm. When He shifts the tide, the plan must shift as well. Faith is associated with motion and velocity, while prudence is associated with rhythm and strategy.

Every group will always have a mix of these persons in its membership, thanks to the Lord. In perception, they are diametrically opposed, but they are essential friends in action. This is the equilibrium we must pursue, the amicable interaction of faith and caution that will allow us to run the next stage of the great race with patience. Faith is not irrational, and prudence is not irrational. They are the movement's left and right legs. If we are to prevent falling, we must first understand them both and then get them going together.

There's a reason for this collaboration. Expectation will accelerate our momentum to the point where we will launch into the atmosphere on its own. We may be content to boldly travel where no other church has gone in our lifetime. Expectation scans the horizon, hoping to reach the pinnacle of anointing and power as soon as possible.

We think on the horizon when we expect something, but God thinks about the foundation. When the moment of revelation arrives, we want to be there as soon as possible. The prophetic power that captivates our hearts is what we are living by. The prophecy, however, contradicts itself when it says, "You cannot go there from here." The journey from revelation to manifestation—the process of transition—is marked by contradiction.

Joseph had a dream that he would one day be able to rule over his father and brothers.

37:1-36 in Genesis And Jacob settled in the land of Canaan, where his father was a stranger. These are Jacob's generations. Joseph, who was seventeen years old at the time, was feeding the sheep with his brothers; and the youngster was with the sons of Bilhah and the sons of Zilpah, his father's wives, and Joseph carried their terrible word to his father. Because he was the son of his old age, Israel loved Joseph more than all his other children, and he made him a coat of many colors. When his brothers saw that their father loved him more than all of his brothers, they despised him and refused to speak to him in peace. And Joseph had a dream, which he told his brothers, who despised him even more. And he said to them, "Listen, I implore you, to this dream that I have dreamed:" For, see, we were tying sheaves in the field when my sheaf raised and stood upright; and, behold, your sheaves surrounded my sheaf and bowed down to it. And his brothers questioned him, "Shall thou reign over us?" or shalt thou have authority over us? They despised him much more because of his dreams and statements. And he had another dream, which he told his brethren, saying, "Behold, I have dreamed another dream; and, behold, the sun, the moon, and the eleven stars have made obeisance to me." And he told his father and his brothers about it, and his father chastised him, saying, "What is this dream that thou hast dreamed?" Will I, thy mother, and thy brothers and sisters come to the earth to prostrate ourselves before thee? His brethren admired him, but his father was aware of the proverb. And his brothers and sisters went to Shechem to feed their father's herd. Do not thy brethren feed the flock in Shechem, Israel replied to Joseph. Come, and I'll dispatch thee to them. And he told him, "Here I am." And he said to him, "Go, I implore thee, see if all is well with thy brethren and sheep," and then "bring me word." So he despatched him out of Hebron's valley, and he arrived in Shechem. And a certain man came across him, and saw him walking in the field, and asked him, "What seekest thou?" And he said, "I seek my brethren; tell me, I beseech thee, where their flocks are fed." And the man responded, "They have gone away," for he had heard them say, "Let us go to Dothan." And Joseph set off to find his brothers, which he did at Dothan. And when they spotted him from afar, even before he drew close to them, they plotted to kill him. And they murmured to one another, "Look, this dreamer has arrived." So come, let us slaughter him and put him into some hole, and we'll say, "Some wicked beast has devoured him," and we'll see what happens to his dreams." And when Reuben heard it, he liberated him from their grasp, saying, "Let us not murder him." And Reuben answered to them, "Shed no blood, but hurl him into this wilderness pit, and lay no hand upon him," so that he may free him from their grasp and return him to his father. When Joseph arrived at his brothers' house, they stripped him of his coat, the coat of many colors that he wore; and they seized him and flung him into a pit; but the pit was empty, and there was no water in it. And they sat down to eat bread, and they lifted up their eyes and looked, and behold, a group of Ishmeelites with spicery, balm, and myrrh arrived from Gilead, carrying it down to Egypt on their camels. And Judah responded to his brothers, "What good would it do us if we kill our brother and hide his blood?" Come, let us sell him to the Ishmeelites, and let us not touch him, because he is our brother and flesh. His brethren, on the other hand, were content. Then Midianites merchants walked by, and they dragged and hauled Joseph out of the hole, selling him to the Ishmeelites for twenty pieces of silver, and bringing him to Egypt. And when Reuben returned to the pit, he discovered that Joseph was not there, so he rented his clothing. And he went back to his brothers and sisters, saying, "The child is not; and I, where shall I go?" And they took Joseph's coat and killed a goat kid, dipping the coat in the blood; and they sent the coat of many colors to their father, saying, "This have we found: know now whether it is thy son's coat or not." And he recognized it and said, "It is my son's coat; a wicked beast has devoured him; Joseph is undoubtedly ripped to shreds." Jacob tore his garments and wrapped himself in sackcloth, and he wept for his son for many days. And all his sons and daughters came forward to console him, but he refused, saying, "For I shall go down into the grave to my son mourning." As a result, his father cried for him. And the Midianites sold him to Potiphar, a Pharaoh's officer and captain of the guard in Egypt.

They were all bowing down to him in the dream. This prophecy was subsequently fulfilled, but not until the exact opposite had happened. Instead of his family staring up at him after he told them about his dreams, Joseph found himself in a hole looking up at them! He was sold as a slave and shipped to a foreign land in chains. His life had taken a very different path than he had anticipated. Clearly, the Lord was not going to fulfill the prophecy because of some bumbling young man who couldn't keep his mouth shut in the presence of some enraged brethren! The training comes after the calling. After receiving significant prophetic input into our lives, we must go through a period of development before the word may be brought to fruition. In his own life, David encountered a similar set of conditions at work. Samuel, the prophet, anointed him as king. Nothing said or done at the time informed David that he would be discredited and forced to dwell in caves in the desert before the prophet's prophecy was fulfilled.

6:6-8 (Exodus) So say to the children of Israel, "I am the LORD, and I will deliver you from the Egyptians' burdens, and I will free you from their bonds," and "I will redeem you with a stretched-out arm and great judgments," and "I will take you to be my people, and I will be your God," and "ye shall know that I am the LORD your God, who delivers you from the Egyptians' burdens." And I will bring you into the land, which I promised to give to Abraham, Isaac, and Jacob, and which I will give you as an inheritance: I am the LORD.

The verses made no mention of their trip into the wilderness or God's subsequent testing as part of the path to fulfillment. This is a crucial aspect of the prophetic and transitional process. Before we may realize our destiny, we must meet all of the character standards that are essential if we are to represent the God of Heaven. As a condition for the fulfillment of prophecy, he wants us all to conform to the image of Jesus. God turns His focus to our character after the first exhilaration of the word and the release of vision and destiny. Now He must work on our personality, temperament, and character in order to elevate them to a level of accepted reliability. Our fate is postponed till we have shown ourselves in our character. We are in the skies with our destiny after the prophecy; yet, the Lord is gazing at something else! He's assessing our character and determining how much work and development we'll need to get to that point of high calling.

Our humility, servant heart, reliability under pressure, truthfulness and purity, leadership or ministry ability, capacity to sustain stress in combat, ability to learn from our mistakes, and above all, our conformity to His love, grace, mercy, and kindness will all be put to the test. In the most severe and challenging of circumstances, all of these will be scrutinized closely. It's almost as if the Lord catches us off guard, throws us into a dark room, and beats the living daylights out of us while we're still daydreaming about the prophetic word! At least, that's how it appears. For a time, our lives go in the opposite direction as God begins to work on our character. Most people surrender their vision and calling here.

When their lives begin to run in opposite directions to their predictions, many people's immediate reaction is to blame the prophet. Because the prophet said one thing and the reverse is currently happening, it's easy to conclude that the prophesy is wrong. In this case, however, the majority of accusations of false prophesy are made due to a lack of understanding of the process. Process is a journey, a set of stages that take you from one dimension to the next. The voyage does not follow a straight upward trajectory from the starting location.

The process through which God transforms our potential into reality includes the release of revelation. This prompts us to look skyward in order to discern our fate, yet it is followed by a drop in our fortunes as we enter transition.

4

∾

In the midst of the conflict, a new church emerges

We come to a moment of confrontation as a result of revelation. You must realize that we must go through all stages of transition. Everything in our church that might keep God from fulfilling His promise to us will be scrutinized. The ground will appear to be slipping out from under the church. We'll start to feel like we're falling into our own version of Joseph's pit. We must share in the fellowship of His sufferings before we can receive the power of His resurrection. There is conformity to His death before the release of His life. Death, according to Paul, works in us so that life can work in others.

4:12 2nd Corinthians So death works in us, but life works in you.

Because the two are linked, if we wish to know Him in resurrection power, we must also know Him in the fellowship of His suffering. If God has promised us life, He will first give us death, because death brings life into our lives. It is necessary for us to comprehend God's mind and ways. We will always be delivered to death by God.

4:11 in 2nd Corinthians For we who live are always delivered to death for the love of Jesus, so that the life of Jesus may be manifested in our mortal bodies as well.

"It is finished," Jesus exclaimed on the cross, but He didn't immediately ascend into Heaven; instead, He fell into hell. He rose from the depths of hell to sit at the right hand of the Father. Even for Jesus, "It is finished" did not signal the end of His tribulation. He was implying that one part had been completed, but He still had another to complete. He needed to reclaim the keys and confuse the adversary. He went down first, then up. He descended into hell with a specific goal in mind: to free captives, render the enemies helpless, seize the kingdom's keys, and conquer death and hell.

This part of the journey on Earth was completed, but the journey in the spiritual realm was not. As a result, He had to descend down before ascending, and we shall discover that the same is true for us. During this phase of confrontation, several things must occur. We will not experience the transformation that is required to inhabit what God has promised if we do not submit to God during the contentious moment. The next thing that will happen is that all hell will break out within the church at some time. Instead of ascending into a spiritual dimension, we will descend into a carnal one. We will discover depths of immaturity among older Christians that we never imagined could exist.

As people's vanity and ambition begin to rise, we will see childishness, irritation, flesh, strife, envy, and a craving for power. Instead of fulfilling our potential for greatness as the church's destiny unfolds, we must come to terms with our capacity for carnal activity. Instead of being lifted to a new level in the spirit, God works on our flesh, and we descend into carnality. Why? Because God is hell-bent on removing everything that is bad in us. As a church, we shall be thrust into a moment of confrontation. The enemy will try to undermine the vision and leadership. There will be bitterness and criticism. Old power conflicts will reappear, along with old wounds. Because that is the whole goal of confrontation, anything inside us that is unresolved will rise to the surface.

Only by going through the cross can we reach the place where God desires us to be. God will lead us straight to it. He will not take us to the heights; rather, He will take us to the depths. We will enter the grave, and God will take care of our physical lives. The enemy will be active throughout the church, but we must remember that God will use him to remove the flesh. God's blessings may continue to pour down because the Lord will not abandon us. God's benevolence is at work in this continuous blessing. God's acts are simultaneous, which means He is always accomplishing multiple things in our lives at the same time. These activities aren't required to add up. They can all be independent of one another and not be linked in any manner. We've all experienced God's blessing in our lives while also being convicted of personal sin by the Holy Spirit. Similarly, despite internal carnality and a lack of unity, we have collectively experienced God's power.

We observe a nice flat surface waiting for new seed when farmers plow their fields and then level them for planting. However, if it rains on that field, it will be covered in stones the next day. Rain softens the ground, allowing whatever is hard to rise to the surface. In a similar vein, whatever difficult in our life will surface during this period of confrontation. Take heart if this is happening right now in the church where you serve. God is removing the flesh; the vision is still present, and the prophecy was correct. The vision is safe with God, and it will be returned to you once the process is over, providing you obey and submit to Him during the transition. Give him exactly what he desires. We are in the process of God molding us to fit the word He has given us. We may feel as if we are drifting further and further away from God's revelation. This is not the time to contemplate our fate. We must observe the process and begin to consider the church's nature. This is not the time to get caught up in projects, start new initiatives, or commit to new faith-based endeavors.

If we find ourselves in conflict, it's because God is dealing with something that shouldn't be there. We don't know how many people will leave the work during this period of testing, depending on where the church is in the process. Most churches in transition will see a reduction in their financial resources. Finances, staff, critical ministry personnel, and leadership may initially flow out of the church. When things are rough, some of our friends will leave us for greener pastures. In most cases, these folks are unlikely to represent a significant loss. We can't let go of folks who never had our best interests at heart in the first place. Others may be more important to our advancement, and losing them would be detrimental. Some will leave because they may need to relocate due to a work change. They might have declined the promotion or change of job situation if things had been different, but they now feel compelled to attend church somewhere else. Some will depart to seek new employment in the area, and some may attempt to bring others with them. God will constantly reduce us to our most valuable possessions. Of course, for others, the time has come to depart because the Lord has other plans. When the heat is particularly intense, though, we tend to burn wood, hay, and stubble.

12–15 in 1 Corinthians Now, if anyone builds upon this foundation with gold, silver, precious stones, wood, hay, or stubble, every man's work shall be made manifest: for the day shall declare it, for it shall be revealed by fire; and the fire shall trial every man's building, regardless of its kind. If any man's work that he has built thereupon lasts, he will be rewarded. If a person's work is destroyed by fire, he will lose everything; nonetheless, he will be preserved.

We may end up with a church that is smaller in size but stronger in spirit as a result of the process. God's gifts and calling are impervious to repentance. Allow God to hang on to the vision and the future;

we, on the other hand, must hold on to Him and to one another. It's the age-old conflict between the Spirit and the flesh.

There are some attitudes, mindsets, and techniques that must be altered. The Lord will address our selfishness, self-preoccupation, and self-centered behavior in confrontation. Before God is pleased that we are ready for the next level of anointing, we shall all be humbled in some fashion.

The prophetic message regarding expansion should drive us to enter a period of contraction, which appears to be a paradox, but it is accurate. The cross of Jesus is our first destination on the confrontation trail, followed by the grave. To God's satisfaction, death must function in our midst. We learn that both God and the devil have their own agendas as a result of this process. Life, the realization of the vision, and the entry into a deeper anointing and a more powerful spiritual dimension are all on God's agenda. The devil's plan is to destroy all we hold dear right now.

1 Peter 5:8-10 Be sober, be alert; for your enemy, the devil, as a roaring lion, prowls the earth, seeking whom he may devour: Whom oppose steadfastly in the faith, knowing that the same afflictions are visited upon your brethren in the world. But when you have endured for a while, the God of all grace, who has called us to his eternal glory through Christ Jesus, make you perfect, stablish, strengthen, and settle you.

We're not dealing with anything novel; we're dealing with nothing that hasn't happened before in many churches. God's approval to continue in His plan and purpose will emerge out of this season of pain. During this difficult time, the enemy has three strategies in mind to deploy against us.

The issue with confrontation is that it frequently occurs at inopportune times. There appears to be no such thing as the perfect time, but some are more difficult than others. It's especially tough when our church is going through a painful transition while other churches are celebrating a hilarious anointing! As a church, we are going through one of our darkest periods ever, while others are experiencing rejuvenation. When you're in a situation like this, it's natural to hunt for someone or anything to blame.

We will understand present events from the soul rather than the spirit man if we have no revelatory rationale for them. People search for the apparent and interpret it according to their own thoughts and feelings, rather than going beyond the circumstances to discern God's beautiful hand at work. We manufacture things from our imagination to provide spiritual explanation to our own personal actions if the facts themselves are not evident or do not add up completely to address the problem. It's always challenging to see other churches prosper while we're going through trials and tribulations. People would rather believe there is a leadership problem, that there is wickedness in the camp, that we have the wrong vision, or that we are outside of God's will. They are oblivious to God's purposes. As God cleanses the temple of the Church, the same process will come to every church in some form. It's easy to believe that something bad is the devil's doing when something bad happens.

Although this may be true, we definitely need the Holy Spirit's perspective to perceive where God's hand is moving.

What He could easily prohibit with His strength, He permits in His wisdom! God is addressing our carnality and our ability to be carnal. The only way for Satan to get his hooks into the church is through the flesh. For the church, the flesh is a greater problem than any demonic activity. The adversary has a tendency to overplay his hand, making his work visible. The body is far more cunning. It comes in a variety of disguises and hiding spots, and it can manifest in the most unexpected of persons. Many churches aren't yet strong enough to withstand attacks from demons. Their flesh is far too tempting to pass up. Why use a demon's power to cause havoc in the church when a few flesh buttons will suffice? When we allow the flesh-life to continue unregulated and unaccountable, we do an outstanding job of causing disturbance and discord. The process by which God begins to work on our character and lifestyle is known as confrontation.

Revelation 14:30 After that, I won't say much to you, because the prince of this planet is coming, and he has no interest in me.

Confrontation is meant to get rid of all the meat hooks in our lives. The Lord will throw us into a crisis, exposing everything that has been buried under our public mask of spirituality. The body will always rise when the Spirit descends. These two are old adversaries who can't stand being in the same room with each other. The inward battle for spiritual ascendancy is known as confrontation. Will the carnal man be crowned as the overriding power in our lives, or will we be molded into the humility, gentleness, and meekness of Christ as we surrender to the Holy Spirit? Will we persevere and remain true to God and others around us, or will we give up and go on, possibly to restart the cycle somewhere else? Of course, not all outward/onward motions are bad; the Lord is repositioning His people for growth in these days, and there are many new alignments taking place. God attacks the body in confrontation. In our hearts, it is the work of the cross. It's about putting personal agendas aside and seeing that the Lord is suffocating our pride, ambition, and lack of genuine servanthood. He is addressing our sin nature as well as our sin habit. He is breaking us, crushing us in the winepress of His dealings, chastising and scourging our carnal behavior, and purging us of the enmity that looms over our relationships with Christ and His Body.

Throughout all of these hardships and tribulations, the Lord utilizes conflict to fit and prepare us for everything He has planned. Many congregations will not advance to the real battleground. Because the flesh has not been laid to rest, they are still in spiritual kindergarten. Before God can lead us to conquer the adversary on any exterior battleground, He must first deal with the enemy within. In infiltration, the opponent tries to come between people and inject his poison into their relationships. Marriage is a popular target. When our personal life is a battleground of emotional hurts, it's difficult to focus on spiritual advancements in the church. Leadership groups are a popular target.

At work, we have a basic strategy: When the skull is harmed, the body loses its ability to function. In this infiltration operation, any notable or significant relationship will be targeted. People's ambition will be used by the devil to divide and control. He'll instigate power disputes among crucial figures. Unresolved conflicts will be encouraged to resurface; grudges will be given another chance to be expressed; and unforgiveness will take on a pseudo-spiritual form. At this time, long-buried resentments, bitter roots, and secret intentions will all surface. To carry out his plan, the enemy will use any unbroken ego, any unredeemed personality or character feature. All of this will be properly concealed beneath a veil of spirituality. These are all areas of entry when the flesh succumbs to the devil's touch.

1 Corinthians 1:10-13 Now I entreat you, brethren, in the name of our Lord Jesus Christ, that you all speak the same thing, that there be no divisions among you, but that you be totally joined together in the same mind and judgment. Because it has been made known to me of you, my brethren, by those of the house of Chloe, that there are quarrels among you. Now I say this, that each of you declares, "I am of Paul; and I am of Apollos; and I am of Cephas; and I am of Christ." Is Christ split? Is it true that Paul was crucified for you? or were you baptized in Paul's name?

3:9–11 And I, brethren, could not speak to you in a spiritual manner, but rather in a carnal manner, as if you were babes in Christ. I've fed you milk instead of meat because you couldn't bear it before, and you still can't bear it now. For ye are still carnal, for there is envying, contention, and divisions among you; are ye not carnal, and walk as men? Are you not carnal, while one says, "I am of Paul," while another says, "I am of Apollos?" Who are Paul and Apollos, therefore, if not pastors by whom you believed, as the Lord gave to each one? I planted, Apollos watered, but God provided the harvest. So neither he who plants anything, nor he who waters it, but God is the one who gives the increase. Now the one who plants and the one who waters are one, and each will be rewarded according to his own labor. For we are God's coworkers: ye are God's husbandry, ye are God's construction.

The more spiritual the devil can make the flesh appear, the less likely we are to realize we've been spied on. The sham spiritual discourse of the flesh playing "follow my leader" revealed discord in the Corinthian church. Paul saw right through all of this foolishness to expose carnality on all sides. Carnality is a hindrance to revelation. It maintains us in a state of spiritual infancy, unable to be trusted with genuine knowledge and power.

(1 Corinthians 11:17-19) Now in this that I reveal unto you, I do not praise you for coming together for the worse, but for the better. For starters, I hear there are divisions among you when you gather in the church, and I partially believe that. For there must be heresies among you in order for those who are authorized to be manifested among you.

Dealing with the possibility of split is an important component of a church's development. This circumstance is not created by God, yet it is allowed to occur for a reason. God enables power battles in the church so that the true leaders can be identified. During times of conflict and power struggles, we can see who is truly worried about the flock and who is more concerned with their personal status and position. We find people who are focused with their own vision, ministry, and anointing beneath all the spiritual jargon. Church members are terrified of division. They'll make any compromise between groups to hold things together and provide the impression of togetherness. It is approbation, not togetherness, that is at stake here. For focal leadership, who is the Lord's hand resting? Examine the behavior of the people involved to be able to appropriately discern. Is there someone who is dominating, manipulative, or domineering? Is there someone behaving dishonorably behind the scenes? Is there someone going around knocking on doors and telling stories? Is there someone on the phone with everyone, spreading strife and division? Who is doing what is calm, and who is doing what is troublesome?

The church will know who is approved of God in this way, for those who act righteously in a situation are approved, while those who act unrighteously are not. Why? They are grabbing for power because they are grabbing for power themselves. The church must gain wisdom in this area. Divisive times are actually very crucial in discerning who in this group of people is truly "called of God" leadership. Do not be concerned about the possibility of division; simply observe how individuals interact.

Those who act righteously in conformity with the fruit of the Spirit and the character of God are approved; those who act in the flesh to get their own way are definitely not. It's part of God's plan to prepare us for warfare so that when we're on the real battlefield, we can trust that the person leading us has the Lord's blessing and mandate. This person genuinely cares about our well-being and will not abandon us when times are difficult. We know we have a captain in the church, not a corporal with grandiose ideas about himself. Most people who claim to have some sort of anointing can talk the talk, but their actions under duress expose their true character. Infiltration refers to the enemy gaining a point of entrance into the church in order to gain power, which will lead to his following step in the strategy.

The constant attack on and within the leadership has a terrible effect on the soul as well as the church's efficacy. Internal strife causes faith sadness, low self-esteem in prayer, and a lack of enthusiasm in worship. The enemy wishes to inflict as much suffering as possible on the church in order for it to be unable to continue in its current shape. He has a stronger grasp on the church today than he does in the future, so the more turmoil he can create now, the better. Even if the problems are overcome and we stay together, he hopes that enough harm has been done to our relationship that subsequent infiltration is more possible. He's fine with us resolving our differences as long as there's a sense of unease in our hearts toward one another and the sorrow of the circumstances we've gone through hasn't been healed. This provides him with fodder for another day. This is critical to comprehend. At all costs, we must avoid resolution. By compromising today, you are merely storing issues for later. Christians have a reputation for brushing issues under the rug. As a condition for moving forward together, we must insist on forgiveness, inner healing, and true relationship restoration.

In order to complete full restoration, the church's activity, program, and vision must be put on hold for a time. Action, on the other hand, will dilute reconciliation. This will open up openings for the opponent to exploit later. Before the genuine exterior conflict can begin, the internal fight must be totally won. I don't want to engage in a long-term fight with the adversary if there are still grievances on my side. Depression's goal is to make you feel hopeless. It is to inflict as much suffering, hardship, wounding, and resentment as possible on the leadership in order to paralyze them into inaction. Depression stifles active faith by pitting people against one another, making everyone tired and sluggish. Its goal is to bring the church to a point of depletion and fight fatigue. The flesh regurgitates history when depressed. We go over old ground that we believed had already been covered. The enemy unearths the ammunition cache that he hidden during the last internal conflict. Unresolved concerns envelop our emotions, adding to our sense of futility and sadness. When we bring up the past, it only adds to our current perplexity. That is why, without genuine forgiveness and repair, we will be unable to move on from our current situation. Where relationships have broken down due to a lack of love, trust, unity, or peace, true restoration is required. Otherwise, we are only burying our feelings for the enemy to exhume later; any promotion of treason, treachery, or unfaithfulness must be fully purged. Before we can move forward, we must thoroughly repent of all behind-the-scenes sniping and negative fellowship, or we will simply regress when the pressure returns.

We must be cautious if we are more concerned with our own thoughts, feelings, and desires than with church relationships. We must examine ourselves before the Lord, since we are more likely to be part of the issue than the solution. Infiltration has occurred, and despair has set in, driving us apart from one another and, as a result, away from God's purpose. Even if our goals are pure, any cliques that arise will have more potential for division than unity. In these conditions, it's far too easy to become pessimistic, even in a healthy way. Before the Lord, we must all be extremely cautious.

Things said and done now will have long-term consequences. Godly behavior and noble behavior will allow us to receive God's blessings for many years to come. Disgraceful action, on the other hand, will promote disagreement, resulting in a recurrence of internal fleshly strife. Even prayer meetings in small groups can be filled with unspoken animosity. In moments of stress, emotions and thoughts demand to be expressed. We may find ourselves debating the issues for two hours and then praying for fifteen minutes. Churches, iron-ically, have formed basic ideals and norms of behavior as a result of successfully navigating these stormy seas. Our God is a principled God. Whatever happens, his nature remains unchanged. He operates from a set of core ideals that instill bright confidence in everyone who know and walk with Him.

13:8 in Hebrews Yesterday, today, and forever, Jesus Christ is the same.

Core values are what we fall back on in times of relational conflict because they symbolize God's unchanging personality. When our essential beliefs aren't clearly defined, it can lead to debilitating depression. As a result, rather than responding to the Lord, we will react to people and situations. Our core beliefs allow us to focus on God and follow the Spirit's lead. We don't get caught up in carnality; instead, we let our response lift us into God's nature and character. As a result, we strive for peace, love, gentleness, self-control, and kindness. Depression leads to a sense of isolation. People leave the church looking for blessings and fresh starts.

Confrontation's goal is to bring about a spiritual shift in our life, allowing us to mature and take on a new nature. Leaving in quest of blessing may seem appealing at the time, but it usually reveals our immaturity and incapacity to progress to the next anointing level. When spiritual despair sets in, we're primed for the devil's final plan of attack. Obedience It's worth noting that the wives and children of church leaders are the ones who suffer the most from internal strife. Most leaders are accustomed to dealing with stress, strife, and spiritual assassination. Their family will be the target of the most direct attack. Wives, in particular, appear to bear the brunt of marital strife.

The number of persons they can confide in and talk to has been dramatically decreased, if not altogether eliminated. They must be more cautious than anyone else in case an unguarded comment said in confidence is repeated by a buddy who is well-intentioned yet acts rashly. This is only one of the numerous reasons why the church must agree on a third-party individual or group to assist them in overcoming the situation. We need objectivity and a broader view of what God is up to. We require assistance in order to be reconciled and restored. We need to figure out what our essential values are. External impartial and anointed friendship and support can help us emerge with our credit, integrity, and destiny intact. Before we get into the debate, the team assisting us must first focus on character and the fruit of the Spirit. Before we can genuinely begin to debate the problems, each of us must learn to focus on our own integrity,

Christlikeness, and morality. In these circumstances, what kind of behavior does God require of us? Second, the team must reveal to the church God's purpose at this time, so that we can all understand what the Lord is trying to accomplish in this crisis. They must expose the process that led to the crisis so that we can chart a course forward. As we deal with them directly at the source, we will be able to eliminate a lot of unneeded words and feelings. Finally, any unresolved grievances or judgments from the past must be addressed as soon as possible. The enemy ammo must be spiked and rendered unusable. We require a stated amnesty so that prior concerns can be resolved and do not resurface in the current situation. Finally, they must be given the authority to resolve the difficulties in a way that is both meaningful and long-lasting, with true reconciliation of relationships and the restoration of vision and purpose at its core.

It is critical that this external committee has widespread support and is capable of being neutral and impartial. This isn't a Christian gang where we bring our buddies in to get them to follow the rules! We will rapidly sink into despair and apathy if we don't have that external frame of reference. Some people will give up if the issue carries on for too long without a resolution. Depression will set in, making prayer and productivity difficult. Some will abandon their attempts to engage. Meeting tardiness or non-attendance will become commonplace. Because emotions are low, there will be no spark in worship. Some will be hoping that a word of faith would break through the shroud of doubt. We shall no longer be able to generate faith from within ourselves. We'll feel exhausted and discouraged, un-able to continue discussing the same topics. We won't be able to do anything since we won't have any energy. Everything will be a test and a stumbling block. We will regretfully come to the conclusion that it is best for us to go. We may look for spiritual grounds for jumping ship to make ourselves feel better rather than to justify our conduct. Some people will simply fold their tents and flee. Our ability to focus on anything important will be severely hampered. We will feel lonely and unclear of who in the church we can appropriately relate to. There will be a decline in confidence and initiative. The order of the day will be subversion and inactivity. Some people will stop being faithful, especially in the areas of personal assistance and financial support. Key employees will lose interest in their jobs and take sabbaticals. People will withhold their assets until the situation stabilizes, reducing financial input. Many of these people, unfortunately, do not save their tithes and gifts; they simply stop donating! Some people will begin to take sides in the debate or attempt to remain neutral. Rather than obedience to God or any visible displays of righteousness and morality, we will frequently select sides based on friendship. We will not believe that someone can be correct about the subject yet ethically immoral in their actions and handling of the circumstance.

I've encountered men who are dead on about the issues, but utilize the situation to satisfy their own egos and ambitions. I've also encountered persons who were incorrect about the topic but were morally circumspect in their handling of the matter. A person's character is more valuable than an accurate diagnosis when they are under duress. Always mark the people who behave like Jesus in situations where there is a high potential for sinful behavior. Obedience is damaging, leading to division and the continuation of inappropriate behavior, resulting in persistent conflict within the village, town, city, or region.

Even those who left the church early in the conflict will continue to snipe at others from the cowardly shelter of non-involvement. Another column may still be at work within the body, maintaining the enemy's favorite tactics of infiltration, despair, and passiveness. Those who have left will still want to be heard in the work. They will no longer be subject to authority, but they will continue to sow their worldview into the homes of those who have chosen to remain, no matter how relevant or harmful it may be.

This style of behavior is most likely classified as manipulation, control, or dominance. We must relinquish our position in the debate. We no longer have a voice and must cease to participate in the debate. If we are approached, we must remain silent. It is critical to be completely accurate in our thinking, speaking, and doing. We are permitted to pray for people's well-being, but we are not permitted to provide counsel. We must stay out if we have taken ourselves out! God's wrath against this kind of action will eventually catch up to us, as we reap what we sow. Many churches have started operations in similar circumstances and seen the same turnaround. When churches are experiencing internal strife, I always try to figure out where they came from.

God cannot own the possessing of anything if He does not own the acquiring of it! How we begin determines how we will end. Churches that started out in resistance will eventually be humiliated. We must investigate the cause of our current church discomfort rather than assuming we are in the process of transitioning to a more powerful position.

Is He chastising us for our conceit and ambition? Is it necessary for us to perform a public act of sorrow and contrition in order to right the wrongs of the past and create healing and reconciliation? If that's the case, we'll need to appoint an outside team to assist us in fully obeying the repentance procedure. It's possible, however, that the Lord never intended for our church to begin. He was never a part of the split and opposes our actions. We may have individually blessed folks (because God has been loyal to us), but we have never been able to expand corporately to any significant level. Our corporate vision has never taken off; we've stumbled from one brilliant concept to the next, but nothing has really taken off. We've had some success, but no long-term breakthrough. People come and go, but spiritually, we don't seem to be moving anywhere. Our church may have a history of constant schisms and divisions. If we have the courage to listen, that could tell us something. We could be squandering our time and resources on something that will never progress from personal blessing to corporate anointing. In times of crisis, we must assess our past with candor and transparency. We might deceive ourselves and others, but God will not be mocked. We will harvest what we sow. Some churches must disintegrate and close their doors. Whatever spirit of discord and rebellion we have cultivated and allowed to thrive in the area must be expelled. Other churches must accept our apologies. Before being positioned honorably with other churches, our members must be rescued from rebellion and deception. Any proceeds from the sale of property and equipment, as well as the current account, might be donated to missions or invested in the area's church unity. What started out in dishonor can end in complete righteousness, leaving no room for the enemy. Our death must be dignified, or we will continue to create problems in other churches as a result of the behavior of those we have handed away. Receiving churches must be compassionate and forgiving, yet tough enough in their relationships to ensure that past behavior does not become the norm.

God's touch on the body is called confrontation. It's God's hand at work behind the enemy and sinful man, orchestrating the demise of everything that stands in the way of Him realizing His vision for the church. Everything is used by the Lord to destroy the world's, flesh's, and devil's activities in our midst. It isn't all doom and gloom, either. We will see the Christ walking among us, spreading His fragrance and beauty in our souls, even in the midst of the terrible process of transition. The Holy Spirit will brood over our apparent turmoil and effect a transformational process in our life, bringing heaven to earth. Many things will be lost, but we will gain the one thing that will make it all worthwhile: Jesus' love...the beauty of His presence displayed among us.

The constant attack on and within the leadership has a terrible effect on the soul as well as the church's efficacy. Internal strife causes faith sadness, low self-esteem in prayer, and a lack of enthusiasm in worship. The enemy wishes to inflict as much suffering as possible on the church in order for it to be unable to continue in its current shape. He has a stronger grasp on the church today than he does in the future, so the more turmoil he can create now, the better. Even if the problems are overcome and we stay together, he hopes that enough harm has been done to our relationship that subsequent infiltration is more possible. He's fine with us resolving our differences as long as there's a sense of unease in our hearts toward one another and the sorrow of the circumstances we've gone through hasn't been healed. This provides him with fodder for another day. This is critical to comprehend. At all costs, we must avoid resolution. By compromising today, you are merely storing issues for later. Christians have a reputation for brushing issues under the rug. As a condition for moving forward together, we must insist on forgiveness, inner healing, and true relationship restoration. In order to complete full restoration, the church's activity, program, and vision must be put on hold for a time. Action, on the other hand, will dilute reconciliation. This will open up openings for the opponent to exploit later. Before the genuine exterior conflict can begin, the internal fight must be totally won.

I don't want to engage in a long-term fight with the adversary if there are still grievances on my side. Depression's goal is to make you feel hopeless. It is to inflict as much suffering, hardship, wounding, and resentment as possible on the leadership in order to paralyze them into inaction. Depression keeps individuals from practicing active religion by pitting them against one another, making everyone tired and lethargic. Its goal is to bring the church to a point of depletion and fight fatigue. The flesh regurgitates history when depressed. We go over old ground that we believed had already been covered. The enemy unearths the ammunition cache that he hidden during the last internal conflict. Unresolved concerns envelop our emotions, adding to our sense of futility and sadness. When we bring up the past, it only adds to our current perplexity. That is why, without genuine forgiveness and repair, we will be unable to move on from our current situation.

Where relationships have broken down due to a lack of love, trust, unity, or peace, true restoration is required. Otherwise, we simply bury our feelings, which the enemy would later exhume. Any promotion of treason, unfaithfulness, or disloyalty must be totally eradicated. Before we can move forward, we must thoroughly repent of all behind-the-scenes sniping and negative fellowship, or we will simply regress when the pressure returns. We must be cautious if we are more concerned with our own thoughts, feelings, and desires than with church relationships. We must examine ourselves before the Lord, since we are more likely to be part of the issue than the solution. Infiltration has occurred, and despair has set in, driving us apart from one another and, as a result, away from God's purpose. Even if our goals are pure, any cliques that arise will have more potential for division than unity. In these conditions, it's far too easy to become pessimistic, even in a healthy way. Before the Lord, we must all be extremely cautious. Things said and done now will have long-term consequences. Godly behavior and noble behavior will allow us to receive God's blessings for many years to come. Disgraceful action, on the other hand, will promote disagreement, resulting in a recurrence of internal fleshly strife.

Even prayer meetings in small groups might be tainted by underlying animosity. In moments of stress, emotions and thoughts demand to be expressed. We may find ourselves debating the issues for two hours and then praying for fifteen minutes. Churches, ironically, have formed basic ideals and norms of behavior as a result of successfully navigating these stormy seas. Our God is a principled God. Whatever happens, his nature remains unchanged. He operates from a set of core ideals that instill bright confidence in everyone who know and walk with Him.

Core values are what we fall back on in times of relational

conflict because they symbolize God's unchanging personality. When our essential beliefs aren't clearly defined, it can lead to debilitating depression. As a result, rather than responding to the Lord, we will react to people and situations. Our core beliefs allow us to focus on God and follow the Spirit's lead. We don't get caught up in carnality; instead, we let our response lift us into God's nature and character. As a result, we strive for peace, love, gentleness, self-control, and kindness. Depression leads to a sense of isolation. People leave the church looking for blessings and fresh starts. Confrontation's goal is to bring about a spiritual shift in our life, allowing us to mature and take on a new nature.

The number of persons they can confide in and talk to has been dramatically decreased, if not altogether eliminated. They must be more cautious than anyone else in case an unguarded comment said in confidence is repeated by a buddy who is well-intentioned yet acts rashly. This is only one of the numerous reasons why the church must agree on a third-party individual or group to assist them in overcoming the situation. We need objectivity and a broader view of what God is up to. We require assistance in order to be reconciled and restored. We need to figure out what our essential values are. External impartial and anointed friendship and support can help us emerge with our credit, integrity, and destiny intact. Before we get into the debate, the team assisting us must first focus on character and the fruit of the Spirit. Before we can genuinely begin to debate the problems, each of us must learn to focus on our own integrity, Christlikeness, and morality. In these circumstances, what kind of behavior does God require of us?

5

∾

In the midst of transformation, a new church emerges

One of the most important aspects of transition is evolving into the person God has called you to be. God transforms us through the violence of the contentious issues that surround us. He removes our old nature and soaks us in the new nature of Christ during the turbulent process of spirit vs flesh.

We learn obedience via our suffering as we surrender to God's will, and we deliver ourselves to a point where God can trust us.

8:10 (Nehemiah) Then he said to them, "Go your way, eat the fat and drink the sweet, and give portions to those for whom nothing is prepared," since this day was holy to our Lord. "Be not sorry," he added, "because the joy of the LORD is your strength."

We can suffer this heavenly handling of the cross in our life for the joy laid before us. The Father will happily fill us with a bigger presence of His Son as we learn to humble ourselves.

The fruit of the Spirit grows in proportion to the manifestation of

Christ's presence; this is God's nature. Our joy in God grows, and we are filled with the Spirit's gladness, encouragement, and consolation. With our surrender, our desire for the Lord grows, and it becomes a source of joy in our daily life. Confrontation/transformation is a two-part process that God designed to kill our body and resurrect us in His Spirit. We will never fully inherit the entirety of our prophetic call unless we allow ourselves to submit to the Lord.

The procedure worked for Joseph but not for Saul, whose life seemed to be a cycle of contradictions that drove him into perpetual confrontation with God and internal reform. God came to regret appointing Saul as king because he seemed unable to comprehend the significance of the method the Lord was employing to transform him.

13:22 And when he had removed him, he appointed David as their king, to whom he also gave witness, saying, "I have found David the son of Jesse, a man after my own heart, who shall carry out all my wishes."

When Israel emerged from Egypt, the quickest route to Canaan was across Philistine territory. Despite the fact that Israel was armed for combat, the Lord led them the long way around because they were not prepared to fight.

13:17 (Exodus) When Pharaoh released the people, God led them not through the land of the Philistines, despite the fact that it was close; for God said, Lest the people repent when they see war, and return to Egypt: There are shortcuts in the Spirit, but you must be of a certain caliber and quality to endure the fight that you will find on that journey. It is not simple! God used the desert road to transform weaklings into warriors. The church is on the lookout for acts of power that can lead to a greater level of life, love, and service. Every move of God, on the other hand, leads us to Christ's cross, from which there is no escape. The presence of God within us inspires us to take up the cross, die every day, and follow Jesus. The cross symbolizes the transition from death to life that the Lord is bringing about in our lives. God has three techniques for combating the devil's schemes and establishing His own will in the church during the transformation process. For a reason, it is confrontation for a season in order to produce metamorphosis. We must adapt to the image of Christ and become supernatural as Christ is developed within us in order to occupy the lofty territory of the Spirit that is our inheritance.

12:2 in Hebrews Looking to Jesus, the author and perfecter of our faith, who, for the joy set before him, endured the cross, despising the humiliation, and is seated at God's right side.

This must also be our response to the cross's direct work. Things in our lives that must die are being nailed down by God. God was glad to bruise Jesus, and God is pleased to hurt us as well. It's intended to be excruciating. However, when God comforts our anguish and ministers to us in our distress, we shall experience amazing love and comfort while we undergo metamorphosis.

An angel appeared to Jesus in the Garden of Gethsemane as He prayed to be completely committed to God's will, despite the pain that this would involve.

22:43 in Luke And from heaven, an angel appeared to him, strengthening him.

God is getting us to a point where He can trust us with the very thing He predicted for us in the first place. He's working on a transformational project. He's cleaning His house and purifying the temple. He's pruning us, thinning us out so that we can bear greater fruit. We can either work actively toward His objective or unconsciously work against it. It will be a quick, sharp, severe, and terrible death if we cooperate. If we oppose or fail to flow with the change process, we unknowingly extend the process beyond what is essential.

God wants us to see Jesus, which is why conflict and transformation are blended into one process. He desires for us to cling to Him and be held by Him. We don't enter a state of contradiction, tolerate it, and then transform. None of us would make it if they followed each other. They are the result of God's united efforts. Although the devil is at large, Jesus is present! The old nature is dying, but a new one is rising. In the natural, we are losing friends, but in the spiritual, we are gaining in friendship with God. We're getting rid of our old wine-skin and making room for a new one. Communion with God is the first of God's three tactics. God wants to be with us throughout this time of transition. What are the steps to establishing a relationship with God? The first step is to humble ourselves in front of God.

He will exalt us in due time if we humble ourselves. It will be more difficult for us afterwards if we exalt ourselves by refusing to give in to the process. The more you run away, the more difficult it will get for you. God's dealings with you will become increasingly tough. You can either stumble over this rock and be broken, or this rock can fall on you and crush you, as Jesus phrased it. I'd rather be broken than crushed, yet I can't help myself. I want to trip over this monster and fall apart. I don't want something to fall and crush me from a tremendous height. You pay your money and make your decision; mine is to stay here and die now. I want to be more aware of the beauty of transformational change than I am of the misery of confrontational change. I want to have communion with God, so I'm willing to humble myself so that all of my responses will please Him. I want to cling on to Him as He holds on to me on the days when I have to clench my teeth, cry my tears, and endure. I want to resolve to continue with God in the process on the days when I can smile because the agony is only a dull ache.

5:10, 11 (James) Take the prophets, my brethren, who have spoken in the Lord's name as an example of enduring sorrow and patience. We rejoice with those who persevere. You have heard of Job's patience and seen the Lord's finish; you have seen that the Lord is pitiful and merciful.

If we are to truly climb to a place where we have a great level of personal anointing and faith, we must first understand what true connection with God is. Relationships are the foundation of all ministry. Suffering produces power, and intimacy produces anointing. We learn to humble ourselves under God's control when we are in communion with Him. It's pointless to express dissatisfaction. Fasting and humbling ourselves before God is the most positive thing we can do in a conflict. Then we ask the Lord to shed His light in our lives. Is there anything in our lives that He doesn't approve of? We learn how to live in the character of Jesus through the process of developing communion.

12:30 Mark And thou must love the Lord thy God with all of thy heart, soul, mind, and strength: this is the first commandment.

The fruit of the Spirit is established at that time of communion. People talk about talents and power when they should be talking about fruit and character in a time of conflict, which I find fascinating. That is the nature of confrontation; it is always about fruit and character, about Jesus' life rather than his power. It's always about Jesus' life, never about Jesus' work. God is speaking to us about fruit and character when we are confronted, when we are under duress. The Lord brings a new level of intimacy into our lives through communion. One of the most intimate responses we can make to God is to stand still beneath His hand, wanting His will to be done regardless of the cost to ourselves. Kneeling to kiss the hurting hand establishes a sacred closeness that genuinely honors the Lord. When we choose to surrender to the Lord in the midst of affliction, it is because our hearts yearn for connection and communion with Him. A new degree of prayer that develops from a broken and contrite heart is a part of that intimacy. We give God permission to touch anything in our lives, and we pray for His faithfulness to last so that His will be done. Our act in front of God moves us closer to godliness and righteousness when we are in communion. The character of Jesus becomes the focal point of our desire to be converted into his likeness.

Romans 12:1 By God's mercies, I implore you, brethren, to

present your bodies as a living sacrifice, holy and pleasing to God, as is your proper duty. And do not be conformed to this world, but be changed by the renewing of your mind, so that you may demonstrate what is God's good, acceptable, and perfect will.

Every day, we accept His kindness by surrendering ourselves to Him and asking for mental rejuvenation in order to undergo metamorphosis. The presence of God in transformation is as abundant as the agony and difficulty of confrontation. The adversity of our circumstances assaults our brains, but as we humble ourselves before His mercy, His thinking renews our minds. We have one more day to demonstrate God's will in transition. We learn to live in day-tight containers before Him in connection. We gradually begin to experience the newness of life that God re-creates inside us when we offer ourselves at the start of a new day.

Lamentations 3:21-26 Lament This comes to mind, and thus I have hope. We are not consumed because of the LORD's mercies, since his compassions never fail. Every morning they are new: amazing is thy faithfulness. My soul declares, "The LORD is my portion; therefore will I hope in him." The LORD is gracious to those who wait for him, to those who seek him. It is desirable for a man to both hope and silently wait for the LORD's salvation.

He becomes the key concern in the transition process as we mature in our intimate connection with the Lord. We learn to understand and enjoy the gain of transition rather than lingering on the pain and loss. God's presence begins to grow stronger around us. Worship starts to grow and reach new heights. Every church should compose songs that express God's love in the midst of adversity. Every church should keep a journal that records the prophecies, vision statement, and mission of the church, which together form our corporate revelation and destiny. A chronicle of God's interactions with the church during the transition period should be added to it. In our hearts, we should make unity a priority. We need to rally around Jesus' love and seek the Holy Spirit to help us discover fresh ways to love and care for one another. This will bring us to the next stage of God's plan.

By the Spirit, the church is God's dwelling place. He is present in our interactions, not in our meetings. The love (or lack thereof) between God's people is what draws Him to us or keeps Him away.

1 Peter 2:4–8 Coming as a living stone, rejected by men but chosen by God and valuable, you, too, are being built up a spiritual home, a holy priesthood, to offer up spiritual sacrifices suitable to God through Jesus Christ. As a result, the scripture says, "Behold, I lay in Sion a chief corner stone, elect, precious: and he who believeth on him shall not be ashamed." To you who believe, he is precious: but to those who disobey, the stone that the builders denied is made the head of the corner, and a stone of stumbling, and a rock of offence, even to them who stumble at the word, being disobedient: wherefore they were also destined.

Paul writes to the Ephesians in Ephesians 2:19-22. Now ye are no longer strangers and foreigners, but fellowcitizens with the saints and members of God's household; and are built upon the foundation of the apostles and prophets, Jesus Christ himself being the chief corner stone; in whom all the building fitly framed together groweth unto a holy temple in the Lord: in whom also ye are built together for a habitation of God through the Spirit.

The Lord intended the confrontation/transformation process to increase the degree of fit between God's people. Our lives are shaped and dressed in transition so that we can successfully fit in with others. Transition straightens us out and smooths off all of our rough edges, allowing true unity to emerge. Carnality and independence are destroyed in the process, allowing God's love to bind us together in a new bond of love and friendship. It is critical to the Lord's goals that we redefine our covenant as people gathered together to serve God's purposes. As a result of the transition, a new set of core values principles of loving relationships should emerge, which we may refer to in times of struggle to ensure that we never again fall prey to friction and divisiveness. Coming out of transition and into a new place before God as a church requires redefining our covenant walk together and re-establishing our basic values. During this time of change, the entire church (or as many as remain!) must discuss themes of friendship and loving connections together.

We must carefully consider what we want from our relationships and enter into a new level of covenant. We must deepen the links that bind us together wherever our hearts are united with others. Friends must express their love for one another and their desire for a stronger heart connection in an open and honest manner. As we expand our circle to include new people, existing connections must become more inclusive. There should be no one who is lonely. In order to evolve a connected lifestyle, those who are loners must be loved into submitting that half of their character. We are unable to alter people's personalities. Some people are more outgoing and gregarious by nature. However, in order to establish a habitation for the Lord, we must all make relational modifications.

Openness and honesty must be redefined, as well as unwavering love in the face of adversity, thinking the best of one another, making bad fellowship and criticism an offense against the house, looking out for one another, and prioritizing others. Make every effort to welcome God! Redefine the church's servant-spirit heart; talk about love and unity, sacrifice, mutual trust, and corporate obedience to God. Come to the place of the early Church, where everyone was of one mind, one heart, and one accord. Make sure that God's presence, not just His power, is your first priority. When a covenant is made and kept, God is present. He will put our covenant to the test, so be ready. We want to create a church that is so appealing to God that He won't be able to ignore it. Only in the midst of adversity can a covenant like this be formed. We can design covenant at any moment, but only amid difficulty can it be made actual. It must be put to the test. In the

Lord's house, true fellowship and covenant are forged in the midst of suffering. Testing may make or ruin a project. We must ensure that our relationships are strong enough to both draw God's presence and withstand the warfare that our corporate anointing will elicit. In this new dimension, we will all be attacked. That is all part of the adventure and pleasure of walking with God in a new area. We get to see His grandeur and supremacy on a whole new level. We must learn to unite and fight for one another (rather than against one another!).

22:28 in Luke You are those who have stayed with me through my temptations.

If our problems drive us apart, it's often because we didn't have many relationships or friendships to begin with. In times of risk, difficulty, and variety, true covenant is defined. In partnerships, it is an unspoken rule that all friendships will be put to the test. We need to figure out who our true pals are. Which friendships are simply on the surface? Which partnerships are built on the basis of performance? People flock to me when I'm doing well and successful, but do I have any true friends who will ride out the storm with me if the wheels come off my wagon? When everything is going well, we tend to create vows or statements of love and friendship. Storms in our relationships indicate whether or not our hearts are sincere. That is why God is fighting with the enemy within, with our carnality, in order to raise us to the point where we can make covenant with one another and live it out. When God is sifting individuals out on the inside of the church, the one thing He will seek to establish in that particular church is covenant. That is what our current sorrow is all about; it is about us individually and collectively entering into closer connection with God in the home of God. In times of trouble, he'll want to establish a covenant. The enemy desires to divide us, infiltrate, demoralize, corrupt our relationships, divide, dominate, and shut down the church. God wants us to join together, start standing together, and renew our commitment with the Lord's house. We must re-define covenant in our midst while we are under trouble.

Start looking at it right now, rather than waiting until everything is in order. What is the covenanting process? Don't wait for things to improve before acting, because we may be irreparably split by then. Making covenant with one another is the only way we can move forward in this time of turmoil and hostile onslaught. We choose to believe the best about each other, to stand together, and to recognize that this is all about the cross and nothing else, and that we must let God deal with our hearts. In our friendships, re-establishing God's core values will become a matter of policy. One of our most important core values must be that we love one another no matter what. Another is that our love is non-negotiable in times of stress and difficulty. So, if we have disagreements about leadership, our love is never a bargaining chip. We stay together because we love each other no matter what. We're just having a disagreement, but we're completely committed to one other. A core value and principle is to love one another. We live in relationships based on God's principles rather than a worldly value system.

Success, riches, position, status, good looks, and charisma are all valued in the world. If those components in the world dwindle, friendships may suffer as a result. God loves us because He is a principled being. He operates in the same way toward us every time. From the beginning to the end, God's lovingkindness is unending. Every morning it is new. He forgets and forgives. He is gentle and gracious, slow to anger and quick to bless. Because of His mercy and kindness, we are able to apologize and change.

In our life, he exhibits the fruit of the Spirit! This is how God treats us in good and bad times, when we are doing well and when we are doing poorly. What makes us think we're any different from Him? We must re-define our essential values in times of demoralization and stress, because they are what will keep us going through the storm.

They are what will keep us from falling into depravity and sin; they are what will keep us from dividing and breaching our covenant with God's house. We're forming bonds of mutual trust and honesty, openness and obedience to God, integrity, love, and unity, all while maintaining a fiery spirit toward one another. We are living a life of self-sacrifice and commitment to one another. We are speaking up, living out, and working out those ideals in the midst of the violence in which we find ourselves. As a church, we will find who is truly connected to us in heart and who is connected to the elation of what is happening in the meetings when we are in sorrow. When churches grow spiritually, they see an inflow, or an increase in the number of persons who join. Everyone wants to be in the presence of the anointing.

Every time there is expansion, there is a period of contraction. Wait for the storm to arrive. Then watch to see who stays faithful while God prunes the work. It is a biblical notion that following a period of abundant fruit, we must prune in order to maximize our chances of future success. After the pruning has been done, see who is left. Anyone else was merely hanging around; these are your true disciples. All the spiritual nomads emerge out the woodwork during times of blessing. They will vanish in the face of adversity. This type of poisoning is known as "felt-led" poisoning. People "feel led" to join us during times of blessing; they "feel led" to leave us during times of difficulty. People like these have no roots and will never flourish. They're clouds that aren't raining. They appear to be gods, but they lack power. There will be no fruit if there is no root. We can't rely on them at all. Of course, we do not doubt God's ability to change such people. Counting Christians does not begin until the storm has passed! These folks have no notion of self-sacrifice or loyalty. Instead of digging their own well, they continue to drink from someone else's. It is in the midst of adversity that we discover the true meaning of covenant. We will never be able to put down roots if all we do when things become bad is go somewhere else.

The leaders will be particularly vulnerable during the transition. They will be the primary focus of demonic attack from the outside, as well as fleshly involvement from within the church. At this time, they require love, support, and prayer. Criticism, complaints, and allegations are more likely to be directed against them. They will be attacked in a variety of subtle ways. Internally, some people may try to undermine their leadership, authority, and gifting in order to gain control. This frequently comes from inside the leadership, a specific ministry within the church, or someone who feels his gifting and ministry has not been promoted as much as he would like. Then there are the vultures who prey on these circumstances among other church leaders and ministries. On the surface, they appear to give a sympathetic ear and a shoulder to weep on, along with prayer and "prophetic counsel." It appears caring on the surface, but behind it is a grasping power. They'll deny taking sheep and merely claim that they're producing healthier grass. A thief is a thief is a thief is a thief is a thief The majority of this activities takes place in private and in secrecy. I feel we should be cautious about inviting people from other churches in the area to join us. We don't want to deny individuals the right to continue on in God's plan; yet, we must ensure that it is God's plan. It's not a good idea to steal sheep. Out of the world, create some new ones. Transfer growth is rarely successful. Unless we have a move of God upon them, it can take years to work things out with folks. It's preferable to eat fresh fish than to eat the fish of others. I am aware that the ungodly fires of some leaders and ministries have smoked countless people. I don't want to deny individuals access to a healing environment. They must, however, be willing to be healed, delivered, and go on in God's plan. A spirit of accusation is despatched to attack the leadership during change. In this type of situation, we must once again rely on our underlying principles. Because most leaders have never traveled this journey before, they will make mistakes. Mistakes made as a result of inexperience and inadequacy are common, understandable, and easily forgiven.

Protect your leaders from both the flesh and the devil. Keep an eye on their backs. We don't have to become "yes guys" who are always in agreement with the boss. We are free to have private conflicts as long as our love and commitment are not on the table as a bargaining chip if things do not go as planned. Disagree as much as you want, but stick to God's essential ideals. Pray for your elected officials. If you're having a hard time, they're probably having it even harder. People cease praying for their leaders when they are in hardship, which is one of the reasons churches split. Leaders are fragile and human, and they need our love and prayers to protect and shelter them.

Transition is a period when we should express and demonstrate our devotion to leaders. They need to know who they can rely on in the midst of the conflict. We will never be able to battle the enemy as a church if we withdraw in times of difficulty. They will not be correct on every point. That is clearly an unreasonable expectation. They are under a great deal of stress and will undoubtedly miss some details. As we go through transition, God's grace can cover our mistakes. Making decisions in the valley is impossible. Let us strive to postpone significant decisions as much as possible till we regain our equilibrium. The issue of transition is one of character. In this time of upheaval, our leaders are taking hits. They're in desperate need of a prayer shield. They need pals they can confide in, people who can help them patch up their flaws. Before this thing is through, leaders will require constant professions of affection. Despite looks, their self-assurance may be shaky. The transitional violence might endure for months. The strain will be immense, and leaders, like everyone else, will need a safe place to let off steam. We don't have to be weird and fawn all over strangers. This is also not an opportunity to infiltrate any future power structure. It's romantic love for the sake of romantic love. It represents God's desire to bless, restore, and support people. Our leaders need the Aarons and Hurs to hold up their arms in times of constant stress, just as they did for Moses in the struggle against a crafty opponent in Exodus 17:8-13. Then Amalek appeared, and they battled Israel in Rephidim. And Moses said to Joshua, "Select us out men, and go forth, fight with Amalek; tomorrow I will stand on the top of the hill, holding the rod of God in my hand." So Joshua battled Amalek as Moses had instructed him, and Moses, Aaron, and Hur walked up to the top of the hill. And it came to pass that when Moses raised his hand, Israel won; but when he lowered his hand, Amalek won. But Moses' hands were heavy, so they placed a stone under him and sat him there; and Aaron and Hur stayed up his hands, one on one side and the other on the other, and his hands remained firm till the sun set. With the edge of the sword, Joshua displeased Amalek and his people.

Leaders need to know that God is watching over them and that others are hoping for the best and praying for them. As we gain ground, our commitment to the leadership in transition will allow us to acquire the authority needed for future combat. We're defending the area we have now, but we're also building the authority we'll need to expand our territory in the future. In the changeover between leaders and the church, something is formed. This is where God tests our trustworthiness by throwing us into the midst of the region's true war for supremacy. Stand firm in your commitment. Keep your commitments to the Lord, the vision, the home, and the leadership. The enemy will try to make you respond to leaders in a passive manner. Actively express yourself. When serving, be visible. Make it a pleasure for leaders to be in charge of the church. Allow your yes to be a verbal yes! The depth of the impression is enhanced by expression. Our ability to remain united in the face of change will enhance our corporate character, resulting in a stronger flow of sanctification and holiness. As we earn a place of confidence with Almighty God, this is where we shall begin to dominate.

Outside friends who can provide objective support and care will be needed as we shift. We also require access to people who are familiar with transitions and processes. In this season of transition, we're re-digging the church's foundations so that the Lord might construct a bigger structure and unleash a greater dynamic of corporate power and identity. Apostles and prophets are the only ones who can truly assist us right now. They are ministry foundations. It is unavoidable that our structures shift during times of transformation. As God transforms us from a stereotype to a prototype church, new paradigms must emerge. Change is unavoidable. To re-develop the base and framework of the work, prophetic insight and apostolic strategy must be combined. External assistance will be required to grow our basic principles and redefine our friendships. For a season, we must suspend as much of our program as we are able in favor of gatherings that will strengthen, support, and sustain us through the process of transition. If the quality of our interactions does not improve, our company's reputation will suffer. Unity is something that must be cultivated. Trust must be established on a deeper level. These outside ministries are necessary for us to be able to work through our differences. We don't just need building ministries on the public platform. It's something we're talking about at the top. A prophetic input from a building prophet is required to describe the new wineskin. There are blessed prophets who are adept at speaking and prophesying over people in public gatherings. Only a prophet of construction can speak of the future in the midst of chaos and urge people to stick together. During this difficult time, a building prophet will make himself available to counsel, advise, and continually inspire the church. The eye of the storm is the apostles and prophets working together to restore peace and order to the chaos. They act as a spur for innovation. They can provide the building blocks to help us to bridge the gap between where we are now and where we aim to be through teaching, guidance, prophecy, and impartation.

6

∽

In Manifestations, a New Church Emerges

All transition stages come to a close at this stage. All that God has promised is fulfilled in the manifestations. It's the most glorious of all transitional periods. The combined resources of the apostle and prophet will lead us to the place in God where the Spirit realm is released. Our corporate identity will be liberated during this time of transition, and a new life message will emerge. Manifestation is the completion and revelation of everything that God revealed to us in revelation at the beginning of the process.

The Lord now has enough faith in us to cause us to stand up and take up a new position. Our character has grown before God as a result of transformation, giving Him confidence in our ability to live at this new level. He gave us the original word, then threw us into conflict and transformation so that our character could rise to the point where it could be released. We must now conform to the message we have received, and a new world of power and anointing will be shown to us. We can't just pray away God's presence; we have to draw Him in by the quality of our interactions.

We must become living stones that fit together to form God's house. Great meetings aren't what the Lord is searching for. He's on the lookout for a home. He will come if we create it! We are made lovely in the eyes of the Lord via metamorphosis. He is drawn to us because of our holiness and love for one another. The Holy Spirit is drawn to unity because it is a benefit. Disunity has a curse that invites the demonic. Because we are becoming more in love with Jesus, worship begins to blossom in our midst. In our midst, our corporate identity and vision are re-established, and we are given a season of supernatural acceleration. A quickening spirit is released, hastening the new spiritual growth we require in order to occupy this new location. As God devotes Himself to manifestation in our midst, time that we thought would be lost and spent in transition is suddenly magically made up. In the Spirit, people begin to expand and accelerate. As people hear the Lord in a new manner, faith begins to grow in their hearts. We reach a point in our careers where souls begin to enter the Kingdom. Individuals have an anointing to witness, and the church has an anointing to gather the crop that God is truly providing us. We shall discover that all of the people God has been preparing in our midst, unbeknownst to us, begin flocking to the church and discovering the Lord.

God begins digging wells for us in housing developments where we have never been. He grants us property in places where we had never considered relocating. Suddenly, all kinds of things start to happen all around us. God begins to give us our inheritance, as well as the land.

In both the natural and spiritual realms, he expands our boundaries. Our territory suddenly expands because, in the face of opposition, God converted us and now trusts us, effectively marking out our inheritance and territory. The initial territorial spirit is God. The adversary is a carbon replica. God has a strong sense of ownership.

11:24 (Deuteronomy) Every place where your feet tread shall be yours: from the wilderness and Lebanon, from the river, the Euphrates, all the way to the furthest sea shall be your coast.

At work, that's a territorial attitude. The devil has never come up with anything new. He does nothing but imitate God. Because God is a territorial spirit, the devil aspires to be one, too. We will get our inheritance from God, and our region will begin to expand. Everything we encounter now will be the result of transition warfare. Don't be afraid of this entire process, which God delights in; He knows where it will lead us. He'll take us step by step through it. We shall come to know God in ways we never imagined we would during our lives. I've spent a lot of time working with churches in transition, and I really enjoy it. It strikes me as astonishing. It's amazing to assist congregations in seeing God in ways they've never seen Him before. They begin to encounter God and come to the realization that nothing can harm them. Nothing has the power to harm them. This is the place in their hearts where their anointing for warfare and struggle is born. We begin to understand what it means to rely on God's presence and on God's person. When we make room for the King of kings, His presence gives us enormous heart and faith, allowing us to continue on through change. When He appears, it will be with power and faith. Even God's whispers will elicit a surge of trust. When God's presence descends, everything descends with Him.

We will grow into a church that moves in God's apparent presence. But first, we must be conformed to His image, which can only be accomplished via confrontation. The prophecy and vision that we received in revelation are now starting to come to fruition. Divine synchronicity begins to manifest. God is present and in command!

Some people will abandon us in the face of confrontational violence. Some will be passing acquaintances, and their loss will be minor.

Others may be spiritual, financial, and relational leaders and ministry significant people in the endeavor. It's possible that we'll lose friends and persons on whom we've come to rely. All of our resources will be targeted. Whatever prophetic promises God makes about riches and anointing, we shall endure a constriction before experiencing expansion. It's a terrible feeling to know that individuals who should have known better have abandoned us and gone elsewhere, people who have maturity and wisdom yet can't see the meaning of what's going on. Some people quit because they want to advance in their careers. Others go in search of a more peaceful existence and greener pastures. People who we thought were anchor points have vanished, leaving us adrift in a sea of chaos. In transition, strange things happen. People who were anchors leave, and those who were floating lay down roots and become a stabilizing force. Adversity has the ability to change people for the better and for the worse. The devil entices individuals away from their jobs, but not everyone is duped. Some people leave God genuinely. However, many are taken from us, and we are unable to support their departure. The Lord makes the enemy pay for his deeds in manifestation.

Exodus 22:1 is the first chapter of the book of Exodus. If a man steals an ox or a sheep and kills or sells it, he is required to replace it with five oxen and four sheep.

Because an ox is a working animal, it indicates a church leader or a significant gift. A sheep is a symbol for a church member. I feel we have permission to seek vengeance and restitution at this time. Consider those who have passed away throughout the transition period. We need five replacements for every gifted person and leader. We want four new members for every church member who leaves. This is critical! To truly repay the enemy, we must pray to the Lord for replacements on the new level we've reached. We don't want to hire replacements at the pre-transition level. We're looking for persons who can help us at this new level. We are requesting an increase in the number of persons who are capable of inheriting and ministering in the new occupied country. We must make the adversary regret what he has done against us! In the manner of the widow, we must gather before the Lord.

1–8 in Luke 18 And he told them a story to show them that men should always pray and not faint; Saying, "There was a judge in a city who feared neither God nor man:" And there was a widow in that city, and she came to him, pleading with him to avenge her enemy. And he wouldn't for a long, but then he thought to himself, "Though I fear God, and regard man, yet because this widow bothers me, I will avenge her, lest she weary me by her constant coming." And the Lord said to them, "Listen to what the unjust judge says." And would God not revenge his own elect, who cry out to him day and night, even though he has to endure with them for a long time? I assure you that he will swiftly avenge them. Will the Son of Man, however, find trust on the earth when he comes?

He repeatedly refused to deliver it. Because of her persistence, the widow ultimately won justice from him. "Avenge me of my foe!" she cried out. This unjust judge is the polar opposite of God. He is not averse to listening to us. However, we must persistently approach Him and ask that He judge the enemy on our behalf.

We must demand the reintroduction of new people at a higher level. According to Luke 22:1, we must seek revenge. The Passover, which is a feast of unleavened bread, was approaching.

We're looking for resource church members who can help us right now and contribute weight to current spiritual advancements. Continue to inquire. Some of these people will come from other places to join us. Others will experience a burst of growth from inside. Continue to pray till these individuals arrive. Take advantage of this period in particular.

Isaiah 61:2 To declare the LORD's acceptable year and our God's day of vengeance; to console all who mourn; and, above all, to enjoy this new location in the Spirit. Learn to relax and enjoy the warmth of God's blessings. It's a brand new day! The New Church is Taking Form as the Glorious Prototype Church.

7

⌇

The King's Process

The majority of today's Church has yet to discover their Heaven-given abilities and authority. At your command, the Kingly Royal Process anoints you with the power and authority of all of Heaven. Allowing God to guide us through the process of royalty is essential. This will help you get to where you need to be in God faster.

I have a strong conviction that it is time for us to lay our immature ways aside and mature into kings and priests with the authority that the Lord intends for us to have.

13:11 in 1 Corinthians When I was a youngster, I spoke, understood, and thought like a child; nevertheless, when I grew up, I put away childish things.

God is raging against His adversaries, forcing them back, so that Christians can rise up into their destiny as kings and priests with greater freedom. In these final days, God's goal is for us to march as a great army.

When the Lion of Judah roars, three things happen—prophetic promises—that I'd like to discuss. Today, I feel we will receive an anointing for the release of the roar of the Lion of the tribe of Judah in our spirit. When the Lion of the tribe of Judah roars, the captives are set free. There is a release in the spirit for those who are sitting in darkness to come forth into freedom in Christ.

Ephraim, symbolizing our prodigal sons and daughters, would walk after the Lord and follow His ways after the lion roars, according to the prophet Hosea.

Hosea 11:8-11 is a book written by Hosea. I don't know how I'm going to let you go, Ephraim. I'm not sure how I'm going to deliver thee, Israel. How am I going to make thee Admah? I'm not sure how I'm going to make you Zeboim. My heart has changed inside me, and my repentances have coalesced. I will not carry out my wrath, I will not return to destroy Ephraim, for I am God, not man; the Holy One in the midst of thee; and I will not enter the city. They will follow the LORD, who will roar like a lion, and the children from the west will fear when he roars. They will quiver like a bird out of Egypt, and like a dove out of Assyria, and I will put them in their homes, says the LORD.

When the shout of God is released in Zion, it not only frees the captive sons and daughters, but it also plants the seeds of destiny. When the lion roars, they come and live in the Lord's house, and there is a rooting that takes place. Wouldn't it be great if the Lion roared over your family and shook the gloom loose? This outcry, I believe, is still being sounded on behalf of the prodigals today. As a result, I want you to take that as a prophecy. When the Lion of Judah roars, it is a pronouncement of judgment on our adversaries.

The prophet Joel predicted a conflict in which many nations would converge on Jehoshaphat Valley, where God would sit to judge all of the surrounding nations.

Joel 3:12 Let the heathen awaken and come up to Jehoshaphat's valley, for there I will sit to judge all the heathen all around.

Then he says that the Lord will roar from Zion against Israel's adversaries, but that the Lord will be a refuge for His people:

Joel 3:16 The LORD will also roar from Zion and speak from Jerusalem, and the heavens and the earth will tremble; yet the LORD will be the hope of his people and the strength of Israel.

When the Lion roars from Zion, there is a judgment that comes against our enemies, but we must remember that we can only find refuge in the moment of judgment if we walk in humility and entire devotion to the Lord.

There is a summons and stirring of anger and battle as the Lion of Judah roars. When the prophet Isaiah predicts that the Lord would come down and fight for Mt. Zion and its hill, he is referring to this.

31:4 (Isaiah) For thus hath the LORD spoken vnto me: Like a lion and a young lion roaring on their prey, when a multitude of shepherds is summoned against them, he will not be terrified of their sound, nor abase himself for the noise of them: thus shall the LORD of hosts come down to fight for Mount Zion and its summit.

This portion of Scripture discusses violence and elicits a response from us in response to the call for the great warriors to come up.

When a lion roars in the wild, the prey freezes in fright, allowing the lioness to enter and seize the prey. Let's get some clarity on this because it's a military tactic. The lion's roar paralyzes and terrorizes the enemy's camp, allowing us, the lioness, to stalk our prey. God is going to elevate the level of authority in our spirit for aggressive spiritual warfare, immobilizing the enemy's schemes.

A never-ending increase was promised by the prophet Isaiah!

9:7 (Isaiah) On the throne of David, and upon his kingdom, there shall be no end to the expansion of his administration and peace, to rule it, and to establish it with judgment and righteousness from henceforth even for ever. This will be accomplished by the LORD of hosts' zeal.

9:6 Isaiah For unto us a son is born, and the government shall be upon him shoulder; and his name shall be Wonderful, Counsellor, The Mighty God, The Everlasting Father, The Prince of Peace.

God asks us to join Him in the administration of His earthly government, and He anoints us to do so with a kingly, priestly anointing. At the same time, God's government is on its way and is already here! At this time, our faith motivates us to take action.

2:17 James Faith, on the other hand, is dead if it does not function.

There is, in fact, a principle at work here. Our fates have already been determined in the Heavenlies, but we must fight for them and work with God to bring them to fruition in our daily lives.

Let us look at King David's life since the prophet Isaiah relates the never-ending expansion of God's authority with his throne. When David was a young man, God picked him to be the king of Israel.

1–13 Samuel 16:1 And the LORD answered to Samuel, "How long will you lament over Saul, knowing that I have rejected him as Israel's king?" Fill thy horn with oil, and go; I will send thee to Jesse the Bethlehemite, for among his sons I have prepared a king. And Samuel replied, "How can I leave?" Saul will kill me if he hears it. And the LORD said to him, "Take a heifer with you, and say to the LORD, "I have come to sacrifice to the LORD." And I will show thee what thou shalt do, and thou shalt anoint him whom I name unto thee. Samuel followed the LORD's instructions and went to Bethlehem. And the town's elders terrified at his arrival, saying, "Comest thou peaceably?" And he said, Peaceably: I have come to offer a sacrifice to the LORD; purify yourselves, and join me at the sacrifice. Jesse and his sons were sanctified, and they were summoned to the sacrifice. And it happened that when they arrived, he looked at Eliab and exclaimed, "Surely the LORD's anointed is before him." But the LORD said to Samuel, "Look not on his countenance, or on the height of his stature; for I have refused him: for the LORD seeth not as man seeth; for man seeth outward appearances, but the LORD seeth the heart." Jesse then summoned Abinadab and forced him to appear before Samuel. He went on to say, "Neither has the LORD chosen this." Jesse then ordered Shammah to walk by. He went on to say, "Neither has the LORD chosen this." Jesse made seven of his sons pass before Samuel once more. The LORD hath not chosen these, Samuel said to Jesse. And Samuel asked Jesse, "Are all thy children here?" And he added, "There is still the youngest, and look, he keeps the sheep." And Samuel replied to Jesse, "Send and collect him," since we won't sit down until he arrives. And he dispatched him, bringing him in. He was now ruddy, with a lovely appearance, and pleasing to the eye. And the LORD said to them, "Arise, anoint him," since this is who he is. Samuel then took the horn of oil and anointed David in the presence of his brethren, and the Spirit of the LORD descended upon him from that day forward. As a result, Samuel got up and went to Ramah.

The Lord directed Samuel the prophet to Jesse's house because He had chosen one of Jesse's sons to be King of Israel. As a result, Samuel did exactly as he was ordered. The seven sons who came before him, though each one appeared to be a strong contender, lacked the necessary qualities and were dismissed by the Lord. As a result, Samuel inquired about Jesse's other children. He must have been relieved to find that there was just one boy left at home, the youngest. As a result, David, the remaining son, was summoned from minding the sheep. When Samuel saw David, the Lord said to Samuel, "Arise, anoint him; for this is the one." Long before he experienced the full realization of living as a king, the prophet poured the oil on David and anointed him as King. God picked David and summoned him. There was favor in the midst of all his brothers. The Spirit of the Lord came upon him from that day forward, according to the Bible. Because God's ministry came to him, he became King of Israel. However, after being named King, David is thrown into a series of life-or-death situations. And for a time, he enjoys great favor with King Saul, but this fondness soon turns to terrible disfavor, and David becomes an outlaw. He's forced to flee into the wilderness like a dog, hiding in caves. 400 unhappy men rush to his aid as he is hidden in the caverns.

22:2 in 1 Samuel And everyone who was in need, everyone who was in debt, and everyone who was dissatisfied flocked around him, and he became their captain; and there were around four hundred men with him.

They came to David when he was going through a rough patch. When things are tough, we find out who our true friends are. David's new pals weren't impressed by his opulent home or his wealth! At this stage in his life, David's greatest asset was his reputation as a fearless warrior and a man of honor. He killed Goliath by himself and did not respond when Saul tried to murder him. These angry men sensed something in David that attracted them to his side, something that defined him as a strong leader. Yes, they were enraged exiles who were bitter, but they were also wise. They could spot a good leader a mile away. How many of us, like King David, have heard amazing things about our future? Lord, how much longer? Lord, when are you going to do something?

For some of us, the fulfillment of what we know the Lord has planned for our lives has been a long time coming. And we're going through something similar to what David went through after being anointed as king. He appeared to have received everything he needed from God to fulfill his calling, but he didn't have the full manifestation of ruling the kingdom for years. David was in training, and adversity was doing its job admirably; he wasn't fighting it. David was demonstrating himself to be a true king, one who had been raised in the wilderness. David had a tough time in the wilderness. I don't look like a king, and I don't feel like a king, he was undoubtedly thinking.

Is this some sort of kingdom? However, he proceeds to take the rejects and train their hands in the bush for combat. He's an outcast, like a stray dog. Saul intends to assassinate him. He wonders aloud, "How am I going to go from point A to point B?" I have no idea how

I'll ever be King. For a few more years, life goes on like this! In the wilderness, he encounters a lot of combat.

63:1 in Psalms When David was in the wilderness of Judah, he wrote this psalm. O God, thou art my God; early will I seek thee: my soul thirsteth for thee, my flesh longeth for thee in a dry and thirsty land, where there is no water; seeking God early, thirsting for His presence in a dry and thirsty land, where there is no water; not giving up when all outward signs seem to indicate defeat; this describes wilderness warfare. There is no evidence of revival; no special meetings are held, and there is no sense of God's presence. Do you know what the Bible says about water? The Holy Spirit is represented by water. I will make the wilderness a pool of water, and the parched land springs of water; I will open rivers on desolate heights and fountains in the midst of valleys.

41:18 Isaiah I'll make the desert a pool of water, and the dry land springs of water, by opening rivers in high places and fountains in the valleys.

The devils dislike water, therefore when we get saturated in the Holy Ghost, they leave us alone! They prefer arid environments.

5:12 And all the devils pleaded with him, saying, "Send us into the swine so we might enter them."

Because Jesus knew that when the hoard entered the pigs, they would rush down the hill into the sea, into the water, which demons despise, he let it. They'll be in the LAKE OF FIRE one day! Not only is Jesus an expert in dealing with devils, but He also provides for us in the wilderness when there is no water. I'll even build a road in the desert and rivers in the woods.

43:19 Isaiah I will accomplish something new, and it will break forth today; shall you not know it? I'll even carve a path through the forest and create rivers in the desert.

Did you know that a river can't always just flow with water; it can also flow with grace? God will shower mercy on us like a river of blessing if we accept it: As the Lord has said, When the sword went to rest in the wilderness, the people who survived it found grace in Israel.

31:12 Jeremiah As a result, they will come and sing in the heights of Zion, and will flow together to the LORD's goodness for wheat, wine, oil, and the young of the flock and herd: and their soul will be as a watered garden, and they will have no more sorrows.

It's tempting to rebel and throw in the towel while we're out in the woods. Even when God comes to us and extends an offer of grace, we reject it! In the wilderness, we don't desire grace. We need to get out of there as soon as possible! David's life demonstrates that the Holy Spirit lavished him with grace. As we consider what his thought-life was likely like, we might adopt his attitude: I've surrounded myself with 400 outcasts. I'm starving for You, God! I'm starving for Your glory, God! I'm starving for Your might! Even in a parched and arid region devoid of water. I'm going to do some serious digging! I'm not going to stop or stop talking! In this desert, I'm not going to give up!

8

⌣⌢

Character of a King

David is someone about whom I've learned a lot. God chose him as an underdog because of his heart and character. David stayed strong in the desert. This demonstrated his character and exemplified what Paul the apostle said in Romans 5:3, 4. Not only that, but we rejoice in tribulations as well, knowing that tribulation produces patience; patience produces experience; and experience produces hope:

When God watched David's character mature and bear great fruit, He decided to prune it, and He prunes every branch that bears fruit so that it can bear more fruit.

Revelation 15:2 He takes away every branch in me that does not give fruit, and he purges every branch that does bear fruit so that it may grow more fruit.

After a long season of pruning, fighting, training his soldiers, and fleeing Saul, David is brought by the Lord to Hebron, where he is anointed King over the house of Judah, and eventually over Israel. In Hebron, David begins to sense more of the kingly anointing's manifestation. It's as if God is saying, "In this next season, I trust you with more." You'll now leave the woods with trained men rather than disgruntled scavengers and outcasts. You made their hands ready for battle! You were dependable. I'm going to enhance my authority in your life, and it'll be more intense in Hebron.

Do you have any idea what Hebron is? Hebron translates to "four city" and "seat of alliance." Hebron is still a city in the midst of spiritual struggle to this day. When the 12 spies entered Canaan, they eventually arrived in the Negev region near Hebron, where Anak's descendants lived:

13:22 in the Bible And they arrived to Hebron via the south, where Ahiman, Sheshai, and Talmai, the offspring of Anak, were. (In Egypt, Hebron was founded seven years before Zoan.)

Choke, strangle, and fight with death are all terms used to describe Anak. The word ahiman means to obstruct or hamper. Sheshai is a Hebrew word that means "to whiten" or "to wash white."

These sons were colossal figures in the land. Caleb requested Hebron as his inheritance after the children of Israel wandered in the wilderness for 40 years and ultimately arrived into their inheritance under Joshua's guidance. Caleb declared that he would drive away the giants, the sons of Anak, with the Lord's assistance. That's exactly what he did! Caleb was 85 years old at the time, yet he had the strength of an ox!

1 Chronicles 15:14 Caleb led the three sons of Anak, Sheshai, Ahiman, and Talmai, the children of Anak, from there.

We witness the children of Israel dealing with demonic powers comparable to those shown in Anakim's three sons throughout the Bible. We, like King David, must persevere through caverns and wildernesses and fight various giants. All of the hardships that God allows in our lives will serve as resistance for us to strengthen our spiritual muscles. We must stand up and fight back with God's strategy when the enemy tries to choke us to death and prevent us from moving forward; when he tries to whitewash everything so we settle for less! We must fight for our destinies. When the enemy tries to whitewash something, it's as if our vision is blurred and we don't see things as they actually are on the outside.

Matthew 23:27 Woe to you, hypocrites, scribes and Pharisees! Because you are like whited sepulchres, which appear beautiful on the outside but are full of dead men's bones and filth on the inside.

To white wash is to accept it; it looks good; to accept your fate, or to grin and bear it! We've developed a complacent attitude that says, "Well, it's out there, and it doesn't impact me, so that's good enough." There has to be some sort of aggressive display. There must be an uprising. This spiritual violence has to exist. It is taken by force by the violent.

Matthew 11:12 And the kingdom of heaven has been subjected to violence from the days of John the Baptist, and the violent have taken it by force.

We need to adopt a new mindset: I'm going to push forward and set the bar! I'm about to have an epiphany! When things get tough and dry, I'll worship and cry out to God even more. You are still worthy Lord, even if the blessing isn't manifested and the oil isn't here! I'm going to keep fighting for my life! My entire outlook can be summarized as follows: I'm going to serve God! I'm going to be a wild, extravagant God lover! David was in the desert, as must all true monarchs. When God promoted David by sending him to Hebron, he would be subjected to even more pruning in order for him to grow much fruit as King of Israel. It was as if the Lord told David, "I will enlarge you." You aced the exam! Visit Hebron! David would ascend even higher as a trusted leader in that place, vying for his kingly anointing.

When David proved himself to be a capable leader, God elevated him and relocated him to Hebron, where he was appointed King of Judah. Because Anak's descendants lived in this new area, he was surrounded by even more fierce spiritual battle. These evil heirs provided a safe haven for the darkness. New devils and new levels! How would you feel about a promotion that, by its very nature, seemed to encourage a lot of trouble? Most of us would never choose to go through difficult circumstances, yet God understands that hardship strengthens our character as well as our spiritual muscles.

119:75 Psalms I know, O LORD, that thy judgements are correct, and that thou hast tormented me in faithfulness.

King David benefited from his promotion because he earned considerable strength and understanding in Hebron, where he defeated numerous natural and spiritual opponents. God didn't intend David to spend just a few days at Hebron. Rather, it was a necessary stopover for him to mature in preparation for the next leg of his voyage. On purpose, God arranged David's pilgrimage to contain many challenges. He knew that tribulation would prepare him for the kingly anointing from Zion, Jerusalem's capital.

84:5-7 (Psalms) Blessed is the man whose strength is in thee, and the ways of them are in his heart. Those who pass through Baca Valley make it a well; rain also fills the ponds. They get stronger with each passing day, and every one of them in Zion appears before God.

His heart's desire was to please God, and it was the driving force behind him.

After leaving Hebron, King David was anointed King of Israel and reigned from Jerusalem.

5:3-7 in 2 Samuel So all the elders of Israel came to the king in Hebron, and king David formed a covenant with them before the LORD at Hebron, and they anointed David as king over Israel. David began his reign at the age of thirty and reigned for forty years. He ruled over Judah for seven years and six months at Hebron, and for thirty-three years in Jerusalem over all of Israel and Judah. And the king and his warriors went to Jerusalem to the Jebusites, the people of the country, who said to David, "Thou shalt not get in here unless thou take away the blind and the crippled," thinking, "David cannot come in here." Nonetheless, David took stronghold of Zion, and the city of David is the same.

He stepped in with the anointing of a king. So David progressed and rose to greatness, with the Lord God of Hosts by his side.

5:10 in 2 Samuel And David progressed and grew great, with the LORD God of hosts by his side.

Although David was not a member of the Levitical priesthood like Aaron (Moses' brother) and Zadok the son of Ahitub, he had the heart of a priest before he became King.

A priest's role is quite similar to that of a pastor, and pastors are also known as shepherds. So it's no surprise that David's heart (as a priest) and his vocation as a shepherd go hand in hand. He was an excellent shepherd and a dedicated guardian of his family's flock of sheep. When it came to ensuring sure each small sheep was safe, he didn't hesitate. He threw down his life and fought the intruders when a prowling lion or bear approached his flock.

17:36 in 1 Samuel Because he opposed the armies of the living God, thy servant murdered both the lion and the bear, and this uncircumcised Philistine shall be as one of them.

God looked down on him from above, as if he were a proud Father looking down on his kid. Because David had sacrificed his life for the sheep when no one was looking, he knew he'd do it when they were. David had a fiery heart; he was a God-lover who yearned for genuine intimacy with Him. When no one was present, David would write psalms and hymns on his stringed instrument. He was probably also enthusiastically dancing in the fields! God, you see, is keeping an eye on what we do in private. When I meet these individuals, I notice that they have a certain demeanor when they're in a ministry role. They believe, "I'm going to church because it's Sunday." I was offered a job and given a task to complete. This morning, the pastor offered me ten minutes to speak. They also don't pray during the week. It's the same as when a preacher preaches because it's his job. He is unconcerned about taking time to soak and seek the Lord before the meeting to ensure that he has what God wants him to speak. I'll just use whatever I already have on hand. David, on the other hand, was like a priest because he had a priest's heart, which was exactly what God was seeking for.

When we have the heart of a faithful priest, we have laid the proper basis for God to raise our level of authority and anoint us as kings. With the priestly anointing comes a great deal of duty. The Lord talked to Eli (the priest) about his two sons because they lacked the devoted hearts necessary of a priest, according to the Bible. In fact, they acted nefariously. They hated God's things to the point where God had no choice but to pass judgment on them.

2 Samuel 2:11–32 The days are coming when I will take off thine arm, as well as the arm of thy father's house, so that there will be no old man in thine home. And amid all the wealth that God shall grant Israel, thou shalt behold an enemy in mine abode; and there shall not be an old man in thy home for ever.

God, on the other hand, showed Eli compassion when He announced that He would raise up a loyal priest and that everyone left in Eli's household would be allowed to approach him.

(1 Samuel 2:35, 36) And I will raise up a faithful priest to do according to what is in my heart and mind, and I will build him a sure house, and he shall walk before my anointed for all eternity. And it shall come to pass that everyone who is left in thy house will come to him and crouch for a piece of silver and a bit of food, saying, Put me in one of the priests' offices, I beseech thee, so that I may eat a bit of bread.

In God's perspective, a devoted priest is a servant who will do what is on his mind and heart.

I'd want to ask you a question now. How can we do what's on God's mind, simply doing what we see the Father do, if we don't take the time to look at what the Father is doing?

5:19 Then Jesus answered and said to them, "Truly, truly, I say unto you, the Son can do nothing of himself except what he sees the Father do: for whatever the Father doeth, the Son also doeth."

We must search out God's heart and mind. A genuine priest is more concerned with who he is in his heart than with his own goals or how he seems in public. Eli served as a priest during a time when the Lord's word was scarce and visions were unusual.

1 3:1 Samuel And before Eli, the child Samuel ministered to the LORD. And in those days, the LORD's word was priceless; there was no open vision.

He couldn't see since his eyes were so dim. This is a true reflection of his spiritual state. The boy Samuel (who was under Eli's care) ministers to the Lord in this situation, and the Lord's word begins to come to him. When God began calling Samuel's name, he mistook it for Eli. Samuel came to Eli three times, and it took Eli that long in his prophetic sensitivity to realize that perhaps this is God.

3:4–8 in 1 Samuel - Samuel was summoned by the LORD, and he responded, "Here am I." And he dashed up to Eli and exclaimed, "Here am I," for he had been summoned. I didn't call; lie down again, he said. He then proceeded to lie down. Samuel, the LORD spoke to him once more. And Samuel got up and went to Eli, saying, "Here am I," because he had been summoned. And he replied, "I did not call, my son; lie down again." Samuel had not yet encountered the LORD, nor had the LORD's word been revealed to him. The LORD then summoned Samuel for the third time. And he got up and went to Eli, saying, "Here am I," for he had been summoned. And Eli saw that the kid had been called by the LORD.

What happened to Eli after all those years of walking in God's presence? I believe He forgot to lay down where God was present, and as a result, Eli's household had little respect for God's purity. True priestly anointing always reflects God's holiness and is nurtured by being in God's presence.

9

⌒

The Church of the New Era

The Church as a whole is currently enduring a fruitless season. What causes the Church to be barren? We frequently think of putting down roots or establishing foundations when we talk about staying put.

The supernatural was ubiquitous in the Bible. In their depictions of God, both men and women talked with a sharpness and clarity. Words were backed up by anointing and power, which rescued lives and delivered deliverance from occult forces, famines, disasters, and human persecution. The Bible's overarching theme has been the essence of pure interaction and raw power between God and His people. Only the form and style of worship have changed over the millennia, from a crudely put-together stone altar by individual persons like Abraham, Jacob, and the prophets, to the designer places of worship expressed in the tabernacle and temple. At times, such as when Jacob-in-transition-to-Israel finally understood God's desire for contact with him, these places of worship were inspired by a revelation of God's grace, mercy, and calling. Altars were established on the locations of fierce spiritual combat and battlefields in earlier times and places, when sacrifices were offered to God on the burning embers of false gods and idol worship. As the enemy was driven out and the name of the Lord exposed, Mount Carmel and Gideon's homeland became places of cleansing and purification.

The New Covenant was created in the person of Jesus, who became the temple of God while travelling among a sinful and sinful people. He said, "Destroy this temple, and God will bring it up in three days." He was referring to Himself when he stated, "Destroy this temple, and God will raise it up in three days." Between the times, something had transpired in the hearts of the people.

2 John 19 Jesus responded by telling them, "Destroy this temple, and I will raise it up in three days."

In the sight of the people, a creeping institution had given way to form without power, style without substance, and a performance mindset that elevated men, not God. People did things to be seen by others, and many people's lives were guided by standards of behavior. Leaders had devolved into blind guides, poring over the Scriptures in search of prophetic insight. Because their interpretation of Scripture was not combined with worship, the manifest presence of God, and prophetic understanding, those who most desired the Messiah's advent missed Him. God was present among them, but they had not been taught to acknowledge Him. All of their years of teaching and distilled wisdom had left them without the ability to distinguish the glory of God. They couldn't break free from their institutional mindsets, even though Jesus compassionately asked them to trust in the signs as part of their journey to a wider, deeper revelation of God's presence. As a result, the early Church grew up alongside a narrow-minded organization that believed it alone held the wonderful tradition of God's truth. The old persecuted the new, which in turn turned against the newer works, eventually becoming oppressors of God's new actions till the current day.

New motions of God erupting in the earth through orthodox persecution and then settling back into conventional, narrow-minded religiosity mar the Church's history. Only God's presence can save institutional Christianity from reducing truth to a set of rules and rituals, or a pointless period of singing without awe. Only God's presence gives Christians the ability to fight the enemy and mankind's evils with a powerful statement of truth paired with supernatural power. Only God's presence binds us all together in the face of tensions, conflicts, and the brutality that comes with being on the front lines of a war against a corrupt and scary foe. The splendor, majesty, and mystery of all that God is within Himself have been lost to us. The mystery began to evaporate as the temple gave way to the synagogue. As we waited for God to arrive in final deliverance, the Word stopped moving us to worship, and the dynamic revelation of God became a way of life. Worship now comes before the Word, and in many places it has become a stage for people's teaching and ministry. Our churches have lost the art of ministering to the Lord in worship and discerning the Lord's voice among us.

1 & 2 Acts 13:1 Now there were several prophets and instructors in the Antioch church, such as Barnabas, Simeon the Niger, Lucius of Cyrene, Manaen, who had been brought up with Herod the tetrarch, and Saul. The Holy Spirit said to Barnabas and Saul, "Separate me Barnabas and Saul for the work whereunto I have called them," while they ministered to the Lord and fasted.

People flocked to the temple to be a part of God's mystery and majesty. They went to worship, give an offering, and pray, among other things. They went to the synagogue to hear God's word, to have their needs met, and to socialize. The instruction and delivery of God's word in the temple always lead to an encounter with God. It frequently led to debate and discussion about God in the synagogue. Instead of revolving around the presence of God, meetings became man-centered. Even now, in many of the younger churches, if the gathering is packed with content and action, worship is frequently sacrificed. People attend church in search of good teaching and fellowship.

People are starving for friendship in our society, which has caused a lot of loneliness. As a result, it's simple to rationalize turning our meetings into a designer-style environment in order to attract attendees. In principle, I am not opposed to it. All of our discussions, in my opinion, should be focused on God's desire to do specific things and achieve certain goals. I oppose preconceptions that keep us from experiencing God's creative presence. We must reclaim our ability to dwell in God's apparent presence. The teaching of the Word must bring individuals into a personal encounter with God, not just a church experience. Within the structure of the tabernacle, temple, and church, God has always placed persons who would act as catalysts for breakthrough into the manifest presence of the Lord. People should see Jesus when they look at us. They should see His love through the way we interact with one another.

Every part of our being should be filled with hope, faith, life, and health as a result of God's Word entering our lives. To us, God's presence is life. It is unavoidable that we would utilize the Word to relegate the supernatural to a future period of glory in Heaven rather than glory now if we lose His presence or, even worse, if we have never grown up with the reality of His glory. God is eternal and exists outside of time. He has never been a glorification machine. He is magnificent in every way. Everything He touches is infused with the aroma and fervor of His evident presence. He is amazing, awe-inspiring, and wonderful. Our gatherings must reflect the splendor of His immutable essence.

I enjoy reflecting on the Lord's nature and character. He has turned out to be the kindest person I have ever met. He is cordial, compassionate, good-natured, and friendly in temperament. He is generous, friendly, personable, and considerate. He is patient with his anger and quick to bless. He sees the good in people, appreciating their value and worth. He boosts our self-esteem, renews our self-worth, and makes us happy. He is enthralling, gorgeous, and absolutely lovely. He is a conqueror and overcomer who is strong, powerful, and a force to be reckoned with. He is a contradiction: a furious and great warrior disguised as a lamb; the king of glory and a broken reed; a son, a servant, a prophet, a priest, and a king; and a son, a servant, a prophet, a priest, and a king. Although fear of Him is the beginning of intelligence, His laughter makes us want to move around. He keeps bringing us to places of vulnerability and weakness so that we can draw strength from His pure joy in Himself. Our encounters frequently do not reflect His nature, but rather ours. Instead of enjoying who He is in our midst, they focus on our needs. How many of our people take a few minutes during the day to sit in silent worship and awe of God? God, whatever He is, is infinite. It is impossible for God to be anything other than everlasting, infinite, and eternal. He is the ultimate and infinite representation of goodness, kindness, and grace. He is endlessly merciful and kind, and he is eternally loving. He loves endlessly and without limits. The goodness of God knows no bounds. He's also without flaws. He never does things half-heartedly. He finishes everything he begins.

1 Corinthians 1:6 Being certain of this, that he who began a good work in you will complete it until the day of Jesus Christ: He does everything perfectly. He is both infinite and perfect in his goodness. He is the epitome of kindness and grace. His love is total, pure, and unendingly perfect! Because He is limitless and perfect, He is always loving. He is unchangeable. He is unchanging. God was, is, and always will be. Within Him, there is no semblance of turning. He doesn't change. What a welcome relief! We've all been blessed and burnt as a result of the ups and downs of human interactions. I like the fact that God's love for me has never wavered. He placed me at the one spot where I could relate to Him despite my inconstancy. He placed me in

Christ so that as I grew up in Him, His unchanging, unlimited, and perfect love would become a constant for me. He is never uninterested in anything. His quiet is simply that: his. Never misinterpret His stillness for aloofness. He is never unresponsive or aloof. His stillness is frequently used to entice us into meditation, which then leads to worship and the entrance of revelation, which brings about change in our lives. The unchangeability of God is what most affects us! I want to cry whenever I think about God's unchangeable essence. His faithfulness and consistency inspire me to strive to be like Him. By His consistency, He provides me serenity. In the midst of the volatility of situations and events, I sense my heart sinking down into Him. In times of crisis and conflict, I find myself desiring peace and love rather than just a solution. It is a sure evidence that God is among us and that we are in love with Him when we agree to disagree and remain loving friends. God is constantly enthralled by mankind. He exudes an inexhaustible supply of energy. Despite the fact that he never stops working, he emanates rest and calm. In and through His job, He finds rest. I'm never sure when my rest in Him transitions into His rest in me. He took a day off from creating on the seventh day, yet He never stopped sustaining what He had created. The fact that man's first day of creation and life should coincide with God's rest is typical of God. Our first day began with rest, and entering God's rest is an important component of our relationship with Him. One of my personal ambitions is to be one of the world's most relaxed and serene persons. My output has increased dramatically since I discovered rest as an important aspect of my relationship with the Lord. Worship, adoration, and attentiveness are all maintained by rest. It boosts productivity without detracting from fellowship by promoting a God-consciousness by the Holy Spirit. The more we rest, the more work we accomplish. Resting puts us in a position where God can accomplish in seconds what we couldn't do in hours under the anointing. The more rest we have, the more power we have to break through. The more rest there is, the more Things around us are prepared by God's hand. As we sit and rest in His presence, His wisdom grows. It's a beautiful blessing to rest in Calvary's finished work. A major reason of barrenness is a lack of God's presence.

10

~

The Glory of God's Fire

The fire of God is one of the characteristics I've witnessed in God. God's grandeur was manifested through fire as a means of communicating God's instructions to the children of Israel.

Exodus 13:21 is a passage from the book of Exodus. And the LORD led them by day in a pillar of cloud, and by night in a pillar of fire, giving them light; to go by day and night: This was a constant revelation of God's goodness and glory among His people. When Pharaoh's soldiers were about to overtake them at the Red Sea, God sent His angel in charge of the pillar of cloud to reverse positions and go behind God's people, acting as a smoke screen to protect them from their foes. What a benevolent God! And He's still in the business of looking after His own today, and He hasn't run out of novel methods to do it. He is, in reality, the greatest expert in that field.

We must recognize that the grandeur of God can be manifested in both blessing and judgment.

16:18 in the Bible They took each other's censers, lit fire in them, and placed incense on them, and stood in front of the congregation's tabernacle with Moses and Aaron.

16:24 in the Bible Get up from around the tabernacle of Korah, Dathan, and Abiram, and speak to the people.

Then God got down to business. As their screams fill the air, these four guys find themselves with the ground parting beneath them and being swallowed alive. The Lord then released a fire that devoured the remaining 250 rebellious men. The splendor of the Lord coming among the people was a sign that He had appeared, but not with His approving presence, as we can see from this story. In Numbers 14, we find the majesty of God manifesting itself at an unexpected time. The people launched an all-out murmuring and complaining campaign against Moses and Aaron after the men gave a poor report to the children of Israel after scouting the country of Canaan. People questioned God's character, advised returning to Egypt, and even suggested choosing a new leader to do so. As intercessors for the rebellious rabble, Moses and Aaron displayed their expected humility by falling on their faces before God. Joshua and Caleb tore their clothing apart and told the Israelites what they should do. They admonished the people not to revolt against the Lord and advised them to not be terrified, but to believe and obey God in order to enter Canaan. The Israelites retaliated violently. They intended to stone these godly men who had told them the truth.

God spoke with Moses, outlining His plan to afflict the people with plagues and disinherit them, while starting again with Moses and forming a more powerful nation. Despite the Israelites' frequent sightings of God's amazing miracles and marvels on their behalf, God demonstrated His displeasure with their rejection of His rulership and unbelief. Moses' intercession is unparalleled in human history, and his audacity can only be explained by the depth and closeness of his understanding of God's character. His main concern was for God, not for the rebellious people he commanded or even for himself.

2 Corinthians 2:13 Because it is God who works in you to will and to do according to his good pleasure.

The closer the friendship, the more you'll comprehend that person's personality. The typical response from God to His close friend was, "I have pardoned according to your word." God goes on to say something incredible. "However, all the earth shall be filled with the glory of the Lord as long as I live." I believe God is implying that, no matter how much humanity messes up God's planned purposes for them, there will come a day when God will demonstrate His total splendor through a display of all of His attributes.

In Heaven, on Earth, and beneath the Earth, his name and character shall be completely justified. To the glory of God the Father, every knee will bend and every tongue will confess that Jesus Christ is Lord. Finally, God demonstrates His justice and mercy by declaring that all those who reject His rulership will perish in the wilderness throughout the course of their lives and will not enter Canaan, whereas all those under the age of 20 will enter as promised.

While God may show us kindness by not giving us what we deserve, we must never forget that we shall reap what we sow. It is a spiritual law, and sin has ramifications. At the same time, the length of our reaping sentence will be determined by the depth and extent of our repentance and humility.

Micah 7:18, 19 Who is a God like thee, who pardons iniquity and passes by the trespass of his heritage's remnant? He does not hold on to his rage indefinitely since he delights in mercy. He will turn around and show mercy on us, subduing our transgressions, and thou wilt send all their misdeeds into the depths of the sea.

The intensity of God's glory fire can be so great that it might be overwhelming. The splendor of God, the strength of God, and the fire of God are all intertwined. And the mixture can be too much to take.

Revelation 7:1-3 When Solomon had finished praying, fire

descended from heaven and destroyed the burnt offering and sacrifices, filling the house with the glory of the LORD. The priests were unable to enter the LORD's house because the LORD's brightness had filled it. When all the children of Israel saw how the fire descended down and the glory of the LORD shone upon the temple, they bowed their heads on the pavement and worshipped and praised the LORD, saying, "For he is gracious; for his mercy endureth forever."

2:5 Isaiah Come, House of Jacob, and let us walk in the light of the LORD together.

That simply means living according to God's holiness standard as revealed in His Word. He then exposes the idolatry sins that express themselves through consumerism. There are seven significant references to God's deeds in humbling everyone who is proud throughout this passage. Everything we value more than a passionate desire of God Himself is the source of all idolatry.

2:11 (Isaiah) In that day, man's haughty looks will be humbled, and his haughtiness will be bent down, and the LORD alone will be exalted.

2:17 Isaiah And man's loftiness will be pulled down, and men's haughtiness will be brought low; and in that day, the LORD alone will be exalted.

That's God's revolutionary, drastic response to man's biggest sin!

2:10 (Isaiah) For the terror of the LORD and the glory of his majesty, enter the rock and hide in the dust.

2:19 Isaiah When the LORD arises to shake the ground violently, they shall flee to the holes of the rocks and the caves of the earth, for fear of the LORD and for the splendour of his majesty.

2:21 Isaiah When the LORD ariseth to shake the earth horribly, to go into the clefts of the rocks, and into the summits of the jagged rocks, for fear of the LORD, and for the splendor of his majesty.

Unfortunately, we rarely hear Bible teaching on these facets of

God's glory fire, underscoring the reality that a better understanding of God's character and ways is one of our biggest needs.

104:4 (Psalms) Who creates spirits in his angels and burning flames in his ministers:

36:26 in Job God is great, and we don't know who he is, nor can we find out how many years he has lived.

26:14 in Job These are some of his methods: But how many people have heard of him? But who can comprehend the thunder of his power?

If we are to be trusted with the fire of God's glory shining through us, we must be exposed to the same fire in order to burn out anything that is not Christ-like.

11

~~~

Mind that has been transformed

We all have mental battlegrounds. We must allow God to transform our minds in order to live a life of liberty. Satan is well aware of the transformative power of the mind, and he constantly attacks our minds, which are his most important battlegrounds. We'll become servants of whoever wins the war for our brains. Paul told us to think about good things. We cannot expect to be compatible with God if we allow our minds to linger on evil or things that are incompatible with Him.

15:33 in 1 Corinthians Do not be fooled: bad manners are corrupted by bad communications.

We have the potential to modify ourselves and regenerate our minds. The mind is easily influenced. Whether consciously or unconsciously, we act in that capacity. Seeds are thoughts. When strong emotion is linked to thoughts, they become seeds, and conception occurs. If the seed is maintained and incubated, it will germinate and replicate according to the framework of that particular pattern of thought, whether for good or evil. Seed ideas will manifest and come to fruition! All creatures replicate in their own likeness and kind, according to one of the Kingdom's most important commandments. Your thoughts will reproduce in the same manner as their ancestors.

People's minds are difficult to comprehend. The brain is a bio-electric, magnetic gray matter mass that functions similarly to a computer. Our brains are used to think, analyze, and transfer information, as well as to reach judgments. Although a computer cannot think for itself, it can be programmed. The mind, too, can be programmed. It may be programmed with thoughts, concepts, knowledge, and values, and it will follow the instructions. Satan seeks to program your mind to follow his program, which includes lies and values that are diametrically opposed to God's thoughts and ways. Simply turn on the television for a while and see how many anti-God thoughts compete for your attention.

Satan understands that if he can take your mind, your thinking will be off, and your entire person will be off. When your mind is clear, your eye is clear, and your entire body is filled with light. The doorway for God's love and light to flow in and through you is open when your thinking is free and pure. We all need to connect our thoughts with God's goals and His Word, as well as understand how He thinks.

The good news is that God provided us with a manual that describes the mind's marvel and how to use it. The Bible is that book, and it contains essential keys to using the intellect correctly. It explains why, without His divine involvement, we are incapable of carrying out His plan on our own.

When thoughts and emotions collide, a creative birthing process begins in the domain of the mind and imagination. Because Satan is aware of this, the conflict is over who has control of your thoughts.

The mind is a spiritual receiver, sensitive to both light and bad spiritual impulses.

6:23 in Matthew However, if thy eye is bad, thy entire body will be dark. How great is that darkness if the light that is in thee is darkness!

The belief that something is true when it is not is known as dark light. This is an act of deception. The implication is to be wary of what you think is light but is actually dark. Why? Because the mind is the conduit via which all incoming spiritual communication passes.

The mind was created by God to function as an internal processor capable of accepting programmable data and programming it into the system. Whoever programming your mind determines how you think and how your life progresses, as well as what your life will become, or what your destiny will be. Because the core of what you truly believe about what you believe, as well as the corresponding emotions that come from and reinforce the decisions you make, is contained within your mind. Satan will want to gain access to your mind so that he can program it in his own image.

The human spirit was formed with the potential to receive inspired supernatural information directly from God, as well as the ability to direct and affect the mind, will, emotions, and flesh to manifest what we receive from Him in the spirit in the natural world. Consider this: God is Spirit, and He created humanity with His Spirit's breath. Humans have the ability to create and originate thought as spirits. All miracles, signs, and wonders that manifest from the world of Glory emanate from this glorious and mighty dimension.

Humans are the only created beings with a spirit, intellect, and reason on Earth. As spirit beings made in God's image, we have our own thoughts, feelings, and behaviors. Humans have the ability to love God; lower species do not.

139:14 Psalms I will praise thee because I am fearfully and wonderfully made; wondrous are thy works, as my soul knows.

This is also true for your mind. It's fantastic, but it's also incomplete since we need to keep learning physical and spiritual things.

With our five senses, we receive physical knowledge. We constantly add to our knowledge base by seeing, hearing, smelling, touching, and tasting. We develop and use our spiritual senses in a similar way to achieve spiritual knowledge. Spiritual aspirations arise up and we do spiritual things when we approach close to God and allow God to encourage, teach, and lead us via and by His Spirit. We will discover the way into the supernatural realm of God's Kingdom and all of its treasures with a Spirit-led mind. How much more will we seek God's Kingdom if we can perceive it spiritually? Humankind's spirit was created by God to receive knowledge and insight. This is what we refer to as a revelation. We use our five senses to decode information from the physical world, and God's Spirit allows us to see, touch, smell, hear, and taste things in the spiritual realm. Each of us has the incredible privilege and incredible responsibility of programming our own brains, and we will spend our lives according to that programming.

22:6 (Proverbs) Train a youngster in the way he should go, and he will not stray when he is older.

What we program into a child's existence may determine how he or she lives as an adult. Our life will be governed by what we program into our minds. If we properly program our children when they are young, they will not deviate from it later in life. A child may occasionally depart from the program, but he or she will eventually "run" according to the programming. When we are born again, we are supernaturally filled with God's holy seed, which helps us to overcome bad programming that runs counter to God's plan. All of God's attributes are contained in that single seed. That seed will grow and bear the identical likeness and makeup of the original Seed with the correct care from the Holy Spirit and the Word. All of God's spiritual attributes, as well as the resemblance and image of Christ Jesus, are contained in the seed.

3:15 2 Timothy And that you have known the holy scriptures since you were a kid, which are able to make thee wise unto salvation through faith in Christ Jesus.

1 Corinthians 1:27 Only let your conversation be as it befits the gospel of Christ: that whether I come to see you or not, I may hear of your affairs, that ye stand fast in one spirit, with one mind striving together for the faith of the gospel; light will flow into your being and the transformation process will begin when your mind and spirit are in harmony. Harmony is achieved by mental reconditioning, rejuvenation, and the removal of barriers. The Seed in your spirit cannot flourish if your intellect is opposed to the truth. Cast out everything that isn't true in God's Word, and the truth will rejuvenate your mind and propel you forward in life. When revelation occurs and you receive it, it is called "quickened truth." The power of revelation is that it has the ability to rejuvenate your thinking.

Revelation 2:16 Who knows the thoughts of the Lord to be able to counsel him? We, on the other hand, have Christ's thinking.

Because your mind serves as a bridge between the spiritual and physical realms for the entire person, your mind and spirit must be in agreement. Because your spirit and mind were no longer compatible when you were born again, reprogramming the mind to correspond to the thinking of Christ in your spirit is a continuous process. The mind of Christ is deposited in your spirit person. Yes, your spirit possesses a mind that is identical to Christ's mind!

4:23 (Ephesians) And replenish your mind's soul; your mind can generate ideas as part of the creative process. It can also be inspired by your spirit and the Holy Spirit within you, such as when you have an instantaneous flash of insight or an understanding of something you didn't know before. As your mind is refreshed and becomes subservient to your soul, this will happen more frequently. There must be harmony between them or there will be stumbling blocks. The brain will sift and sort the information it receives, but unless there is harmony with the spirit, the unregenerate mind will chuck aside or obstruct spiritual revelation.

2:14 in 1 Corinthians The natural man, on the other hand, does not receive the things of the Spirit of God because they are foolishness to him; nor can he understand them since they are spiritually discerning.

The natural mind refers to the mind or soul life that has been programmed with thoughts from this world and the domain of darkness. Different thinking must be trained into the spiritual person.

2:12 Now we have gotten the spirit of God, not the spirit of the world, so that we may know the things that God has freely given to us.

6:17 in 1 Corinthians He who is linked to the Lord, on the other hand, is one spirit.

Everything that God is already dwells in your spirit person because your spirit has made one with Him. We are one spirit with the Lord and are linked to Him. We need to link the brain with the spirit, bringing the two together so that they don't run on separate programs.

2 Corinthians 12:2 And do not be conformed to this world, but be changed by the renewing of your mind, so that you may demonstrate what is God's good, acceptable, and perfect will.

The Word of God, which you receive whether you grasp it or not, must transform your brain from the soulish notions of the world. There are many things in God's Word that we don't fully comprehend. We read things and then dismiss them because there is a layer that is not visible to us. Whether we grasp it or not, God's Word is true. And it all begins with our acceptance of God's Word, whether we comprehend it or not. It is the Word of God. This is the initial step in the process of rejuvenation. The unrenewable intellect is the greatest impediment to walking with God.

4:8 Philippians Finally, friends, whatever things are true, whatever things are honest, whatever things are just, whatever things are pure, whatever things are beautiful, whatever things are worthy of praise, consider these things.

This Scripture should serve as a constant reminder to us. It should operate as a mental filter that we apply to our thoughts. Reject anything that isn't true, honest, or pure.

8:7 in Romans Because the carnal mind is at odds with God, because it is not, and cannot be, subject to God's law.

To put it another way, the natural mind is God's adversary. This remark elucidates the workings of the carnal, natural mind in shocking detail. When the intellect is separated from God, it becomes an adversary of God and despises Him. Even though your spirit has been reborn, if your intellect has not been renewed, there will be conflict. Because of incorrect concepts, your spirit moves via your intellect, and truth is impeded, corrupted, and altered. If we can update our thinking patterns such that they are compatible with our spirit man, there will be an unification that will allow light, enlightenment, and knowledge to pour into our being and transform us through a supernatural gateway from Heaven. Then we shall be able to comprehend the mysteries of creation and the universe. Because our brains are in tune with God, we will understand Him and His goals. Only when the two are compatible do the supernatural paths open up.

Your spirit originated in Heaven and has existed for a long time. I'm referring to the spirit, not the soul. The soul is the essence of who a person is as a person. A human can't exist without a soul.

It's critical that our spirit, soul, and body come together as one so that we can interact with both the spiritual and physical realms. Heaven began as a spiritual realm. God, on the other hand, created the earth and brought Heaven to it, bringing it into the physical realm. Christ entered your spirit when you were reborn. There's more to that seed than just spirit. You are a living soul, and the mind is the key to unlocking your potential. We discussed living and moving by the Spirit's Law in a previous chapter.

Demons or bad spirits can take up residence in the brain, control-ling or influencing thought pathways and corrupting the imagination. Any pure light of insight that comes to us is filtered by them. When this happens, a person requires help. The demonic spirit realm has the ability to influence us, and if we let it in, it can attach itself to our thought life or imagination, forming a spiritual stronghold. Evil spirits construct strongholds and affix themselves to us as a fictitious concept or way of thinking. They dress our minds in filth, putting unclean concepts into our thinking and bolstering lies. We will close the doors or routes if we refuse them. The more we shut the doors, the more likely people are to give up. Because spirits have an amazing power to connect with the brain by projecting visuals, thoughts, or concepts, we must be careful door-closers. They may nest in our heads and even multiply if we do not slam the door shut.

Our goals and visions must be in harmony with what God has called us to do and where we want to go in the future. We shall begin to fill up with light if we can achieve even a little degree of compati-bility between our spirit and our brain. God's wonders will be shown to us. We shall begin to comprehend in ways we have never known before. We shall begin to flow into our destiny as the creative aspect of our lives blossoms. Many people have a destiny that they never realize or believe in because they can't see it or believe it. Their brains aren't big enough to handle their fate. The spirit is unquestionably vast, but the mind is constrained.

In these final days, God will have a supernatural people, a Glory generation, who will accomplish things we never dreamed imaginable. If we are to govern the world with Christ, we must be transformed into the overcoming Body of Christ. If we want to achieve the "all things are possible" goal, we must first synchronize our mind and soul. When we expand our thinking by connecting it with our spirit, we can have a huge impact on the Glory harvest. Going to church every Sunday won't help, but possessing the mind of Heaven would.

The battleground is in one's head. We're up against a ruthless foe who wants to take power. How do we reclaim it? Our lives must become so transparent that others can recognize Jesus in our lives and activities.

All that Jesus accomplished in a single body, He will accomplish again through the corporate Body as an end-time witness to the nations, appointing some to be apostles, prophets, evangelists, pastors, and teachers to carry out the ministry's task. We are about to be elevated into the spirit realm through an act of intervention, where ministry will be based on relationship rather than gifts. There will be clear trails leading to the hidden treasures of mysterious locations.

45:1-3 Isaiah Thus saith the LORD to his anointed, to Cyrus, whose right hand I have held, to subdue nations before him; and I will loose the loins of kings, to open before him the two leaved gates; and the gates shall not be shut; I will go ahead of thee, and make the crooked places straight: I will break in pieces the gates of brass, and cut in sunder the bars of iron: And I will give thee the treasures of darkness

Straight roads were nothing new to Jesus. He had the ability to walk through walls and had done so. As we grow in sonship and renew our thoughts for change, we shall be able to walk in the seemingly impossible with ease. We have the ability to break down barriers of resistance as well as barriers meant to keep us out. We won't comprehend how we went through them to the other side, just as Peter didn't understand how he was able to walk on water, because walking in the ways of the Spirit's rule contradicts all natural logic. God promises that the gates will not be shut to those walking in the wind of the Spirit, in the power of a reformed mentality, and in compatibility with God as co-heirs. The spiritual sons and daughters of God will be able to pass through these spiritual gates and gain access to Eden's door and the Tree of Life. They are the two doors of destiny that will open for you to encounter God in actual, tangible ways, executing and partaking of the ever-increasing and all-powerful realm of Glory in the Kingdom of God for His Glory. Are you ready to enter new depths of God's Glory realm realities?

12

～

A New Dimension

God is releasing more healings, miracles, signs, and wonders than ever before. If we want to see miracles, signs, and wonders today, I believe we need to function in a spirit of counsel, which will release God's might and power.

Wisdom, understanding, and revelation are always linked to God's power. The healing ministry is aided by the word of knowledge, which is a God-given tool.

In the Spirit, I saw that God had set apart this mountain high spot for Himself, where He will assemble ministries. This is taking place all over the globe. Days of encounters with the Lord Jesus are on the way, including Lord's visits, trances, nightmares, and hearing God directly while lying on the carpet!

I've wanted to walk in the supernatural for a long time. When I first awoke, I was desperate to walk in the Spirit. Elisha had eyes that could see into the skies, and he asked for his servant Gehazi's eyes to be opened so that he might see into the heavens. Then they both saw angels and devils as they entered the second heaven.

Before my Father accomplishes anything, I'd like to know what he's up to in heaven. I want to be a part of Jesus' ministry. Even in today's ministry, it's critical that we use that gift, especially in the area of healing. We need to get to the point where we know what God is going to do before he does it because we've seen it before.

1:17 (Ephesians) That the Father of Glory, the God of our Lord Jesus Christ, may give you the spirit of insight and revelation in the knowledge of him:

I'd often lay before the Lord before a meeting and say, "Let me see that meeting, God." How will the altar call be performed? When is it going to happen? Because I took the time to observe what my Father was doing, the Word of knowledge pours. I called attention to what he was doing, and he followed through. Except for the fact that I took the time to seek advice, it had nothing to do with me. The details of the word of knowledge that precisely defined his condition are described by God. People were entirely healed with no laying on of hands and only the spoken word, he claims. The word of wisdom is such a potent weapon.

"...may the God of our Lord Jesus Christ, the Father of glory, impart to you the spirit of wisdom and revelation in the knowledge of Him," the Apostle Paul prays in Ephesians 1:17. God wants to offer us more than just knowledge of himself; he also wants us to know what he is doing. In verse 18, Paul continues to pray that God's people's eyes and hearts be enlightened so that they may know the hope of His calling and the exceeding glory of his power. He goes on to say that all of this knowledge and insight is due to the working of God's might in Christ, which he accomplished when he raised him from the grave. You'll see that there's a link between intelligence and understanding and his power's exceeding magnitude in this text. God, according to the apostle Paul, desires to reveal the exceeding greatness of his power to all who believe. Why? As a result, we can be confident that the same Spirit that resurrected Christ from the dead is at work in us.

You can imagine yourself as a temple of the Holy Spirit, with the God of the universe residing within you. You can have Christ in you, the hope of glory, but until you move beyond the logos to the rhema, you won't be able to walk in the evidence of that power (quickened personal word). The exceeding majesty of God's strength is seen in the rhema.

The Holy Spirit's actions are always linked to advice. It's the Spirit of counsel and the Spirit of might; the might is always linked to wisdom, and God's strength is found in the domain of knowledge. The power, miracles, healings, signs, and marvels are only found where we do what we see the Father doing and speak what we hear the Father saying. Remember, we are healed by his stripes. Many Christians are astounded by this reality since it is not a quickened rhema word to them. They are having difficulty getting healing now since they haven't seen everyone healed, despite the fact that they think God wants to heal everyone. I believe there is a place where healing leaps from eternity, from the future, and lands on you right now. That is why it is critical that we comprehend the word of knowledge in the area of healing ministry. It's not that God's message isn't true; it's just that we haven't received a heart revelation of it yet. Christians who are unaware of the necessity of revelation frequently take dry scripture truths and utter them outside of the Lord's timing, resulting in death rather than life. God want to speak to us personally through quickening words from from high. How many times have you opened a chapter of scripture and felt as if it were alive to you, as if you were living in it? Others may have overlooked the passage, but it was a real, strong truth for you. Then something else jumps off the page and captures your heart the next month: it's your word from the Lord. I believe God is doing away with sermons and sending these messages directly to people's hearts. He's expanding the scope of knowledge, so it's no longer merely repeating what God said over 2000 years ago, even though that message remains accurate. The Holy Spirit must still be active in the ministry of the word to our hearts because it is the Spirit who brings it to life and makes it real for us. The word of knowledge is this living word.

There is a wasting sickness in the souls of Christians in North America today because they haven't learned how to wait, receive, and act in the word of knowledge. Because they don't have time to seek God first, many people simply do whatever they want and pray for His blessing. While I was praying, the Lord cautioned me to be wary of our tendency as Christians to rely on our understanding rather than the voice of the Spirit.

God is the Alpha and Omega, the beginning and end, the everlasting Father, and the huge "I am." He has witnessed the beginning and end of time, as well as everything in between. He was there before everybody else. He is the one who has been, is, and will be. He is God, and there has never been anyone before or after Him.

God desires to offer us these foreshadowings of the future because He has everything planned and predestined in eternity before the earth was created. All I have to do now is enter those celestial realms and ask the Holy Spirit to breathe His Spirit of wisdom, revelation, understanding, counsel, and might on me.

13

~

The Key to the Country

God is giving us keys to the nations in the new pattern Church. This is the release of a new degree of power and authority.

11:2 (Isaiah) And the spirit of the LORD shall rest upon him, the spirit of wisdom and understanding, the spirit of counsel and might, the spirit of knowledge and of the fear of the LORD; we see wisdom, knowledge, understanding, and the Spirit of counsel and might in this passage. Power, signs, and wonders are released by the amazing counselor. It makes no difference whether you have enough faith or anointing, or whether or not someone places their hands on you. It's no longer about you when you're acting in the world of knowledge; it's about what the Father has already accomplished in his mission. When you start listening for the Father's instructions and hearing his purposes, you'll be able to speak them out with authority. Then, because you've seen what he wanted to do, he does what he said he'd do. You take what God has already said in heaven and put it into practice. It's as though Moses just built what he saw in heaven.

Abraham was likewise a God-fearing guy who understood the

Father's plans. God instructed Abraham to leave his homeland and travel to a location He would show him. He would show him a city built and designed by God. Yes, the Lord will construct this structure, and He will provide us with the blueprint. When we work for God's purposes, it's critical that we do things exactly as we saw God do them.

It is a misuse of God's people when we do not take time to wait on the Lord for His purposes in ministry. We're not functioning on the rhema word, the quickened word, so it doesn't feed the spirits of God's people. Man shall not live by bread alone, according to the Bible, but by every word that comes from God's mouth. There is one more word to come; power and rest are both contained in that word. When we get that word, we put an end to our labors and join God's purposes.

106:13-15 (Psalms) They quickly forgot about his works, and they didn't bother to seek his advice: But in the wilderness, he lusted excessively and tempted God in the desert. And he granted their prayer, but he instilled leanness in their hearts.

He poured leanness into their souls, according to that verse. Because they did not wait for God's advice, God gave them leanness in their souls. They did not take the time to truly listen to God. They didn't believe the Father wanted to talk to them or that his lambs could hear him. God inflicted a withering in their souls and a famine in the book of Revelation.

I tell you, there is a famine in the land today in North America, just as there was before. Because we now have programs and seeker-friendly events, there is a wasting sickness in the soul of the North American church. We now have every religion and every semblance of godliness, but we refuse to acknowledge the power. We have all of the mega-churches, all of the professional preachers, and all of the politically correct people. There are people who believe they are someone because they have a degree. We've got all the enormous carpets, all the big million-dollar structures, and all the professional music. We've gathered everything we believe we'll need to carry out Jesus' ministry, and it all appears to be in order. We have all we need, but we're empty, and no one is being saved, healed, or delivered. We don't see a lot of power, except when a healing evangelist comes in to minister every now and again.

1 Thessalonians 1:20 Which he accomplished in Christ by raising him from the dead and placing him at his right side in the celestial realms,

Our religious worldview believes that it is a certain group of people, a denomination, or a specific stream. As Christians, we are the fullness of him, the fullness of the Godhead in bodily form, according to Scripture. We can live in that fullness, just as Jesus did, who had an unlimited supply of the Holy Spirit.

"You're still not operating in the whole of what God has for you," the apostle Paul said in Ephesians, despite the fact that he was speaking to Spirit-filled believers. He was telling them that they hadn't truly desired the Spirit without measure because they were content and had a restricted view of God. They hadn't been truly hungry and desperate, and they hadn't realized that God intended for them to be powerful ministers just as much as the pastor. The Lord wants Christians to understand that walking in authority is impossible for us.

1:19 (Ephesians) And, according to the working of his mighty strength, what is the exceeding greatness of his power to us-ward who believe?

It's not simply about the apostles, prophets, teachers, evangelists, and those God is rising up in the five-fold ministry, as it was for the Ephesians church. When the Holy Spirit began to disclose this to me, He inquired, " "Do you have any idea how the church in North America should look? It must resemble a representation of who I was 2000 years ago. And, above all, who I was was dedicated to finding and rescuing the lost. You saw the gospel preached, the sick and diseased cured, and those afflicted by the devil set free when you saw me in scripture."

14

~

The National Wealth

We're about to enter a year of plenty. I'm referring to a spiritual season of blessings, not a calendar year.

Every year, the Holy Spirit will give me something new to believe for at a higher level, allowing me to be more focused on where the blessing will be. Here's what I've heard as a major topic for the year ahead.

This year, we'd like to establish a faith level.

60:11 (Isaiah) As a result, thy gates shall be open at all times; they shall not be shut day or night, so that mankind may bring the troops of the Gentiles and their rulers before thee.

Can you envision something like this happening in your company, organization, or church? The gates or doors are open 24 hours a day, 7 days a week for continuous welcoming! The money keeps pouring in. Why? What is the key to gaining access to the kind of wealth that the Lord is now releasing?

Isaiah 60 is an important chapter.

This chapter is divided into three sections:

Harvest and Prodigals are the first two things that come to mind.

2. Presence of Glory

3. monetary wealth

60:1 (Isaiah) Shine, for thy light has arrived, and the LORD's splendor has descended upon thee.

It's time for you to rise and shine!

60:2 (Isaiah) For behold, the earth will be covered in darkness, and the people will be in total darkness; but the LORD will arise upon thee, and his glory will be seen upon thee.

What is the name of the King of Glory?

Chabod = Glory (kah-vohd) Strongs: 3519: heaviness, heaviness, heaviness, heaviness, heaviness, heaviness, heaviness, heaviness, heaviness, heaviness, heaviness, heaviness, heaviness, heaviness, heaviness, heaviness

3–4 in Isaiah 60:3 And the Gentiles will flock to thy light, and kingdoms will be drawn to the splendor of thy rising. Lift up thy eyes around you and see: all the people gather around thee, and they come to thee; thy sons will come from far away, and thy daughters will be nurtured at thy side.

The prodigal sons and daughters are returning home. The National Wealth Simultaneously with the huge harvest in the countries, we will witness a release of great provision when we emerge and shine. Keep in mind what the glory presence entails.

Isaiah 60:5, 6 is a prophecy from the prophet Isaiah. Then thou shalt see, and thy heart shall fear, and thy heart shall be enlarged; for the fullness of the sea shall be converted unto thee, and the Gentile powers shall approach unto thee. The dromedaries of Midian and Ephah will cover thee, and all the people of Sheba will come: they will bring gold and incense, and they will proclaim the LORD's praises.

Those who answer yes will get unparalleled prosperity from God. We know that this is Joseph's anointing season. We must save food during the years of abundance to prepare for the impending famine.

Illegal sex, pornography, drugs, child labor, prostitution, organized crime, and other activities generate billions of money. It is past time for the sinner's money to be distributed to the righteous. God will provide the church with far more resources than we require to carry out the mission he has given us. God will shower financial blessings on those that rise and shine! To succeed, a spirit of insight and revelation is released. What to do, when to do it, where to do it, and how to do it.

God revealed to me that we were not fully developing at the rate that the Lord had planned for us, and that our wineskins, infrastructures, and big-thinking levels would not be able to contain what the Lord had planned for us this year. One thing that will impede us from being wealthy is our tendency to think small. I can't help but assume that for many Ministries, the aim of that is also a focus for the year. Of course, having a lot of money comes with a lot of responsibility. Money from lands and houses is laid at the apostles' feet at the end of Acts 4 to be distributed to the poor and widows. That is the purpose of wealth. Then there's the fear of the Lord factor with Ananias and Sapphira in Acts 5's opening few lines. It was an invitation to a higher level of accountability, faithfulness, and holiness.

Psalms 2:8 If you ask me, I will give you the heathen as an inheritance and the furthest portions of the world as your possession.

11:15 (Revelations) And the seventh angel sounded, and great voices in heaven said, "The kingdoms of this world have become the kingdoms of our Lord, and of his Christ; and he shall reign for ever and ever."

24:1 (Psalms) A Davidic psalm. The earth, with all its fulness, is the LORD's; the world, with all its inhabitants.

Is it possible to save a country in a single day? What sort of harvest outlook do we have? How easy is it for God to accomplish the seemingly impossible?

Investing time and energy in the harvest will only lead us to the remainder of Isaiah 60.

Isaiah 60:7-11 All the sheep of Kedar will be gathered to thee, and the rams of Nebaioth will minister to thee; they will come up with acceptance on my altar, and I will glorify my glory home. Who are these people who fly like clouds and doves to their windows? Surely, the isles will wait for me, and the Tarshish ships first, to bring thy sons from far away, with their money and gold, to the name of the LORD thy God, and to the Holy One of Israel, because he hath glorified thee. And strangers' sons will build thy walls, and their kings will minister to thee; for I smote thee in my fury, but I have mercy on thee in my favor. As a result, thy gates shall be open at all times; they shall not be shut day or night, so that mankind may bring the troops of the Gentiles and their rulers before thee.

15

~

God's AWARENESS

I preached a message on God's AWARENESS when I was preaching at the Waves of Revival in Belleville, IL. God's sensitivity will be increased as a result of this. I'd want to pause for a moment as we continue in the faith, holding on to our beliefs and expecting God to work in and through us along the journey.

For us, life is a constant flow as the minutes, and often hours, pass without a sign of awareness of what we are to be experiencing in God. We are made in God's image and created to function as one with Him at all times and in all situations, ever cognizant of God in us, ever aware of this oneness, every second of every minute of every hour of every day of every week of every month of every year.

John 17:10–11 And all of mine is thine, and thine is mine, and in them I am glorified. And now I'm no longer in the world, but these are, and I've come to see thee. Holy Father, keep them whom thou hast given me in thy name, that they may be one as we are.

John 17:20 I pray not only for them, but also for those who will believe in me through their word; that they may all be one; as thou,

Father, art in me, and I in thee, that they may also be one in us: that the world may believe that thou hast sent me. And I have given them the glory that you have given me, so that they may be one as we are:

As we embrace Him as our personal Savior and live our lives full with His Spirit, there is an unending flow in us that comes from the very essence of who He is. We are so engrossed in our physical selves that it's difficult for us to comprehend that we are first and foremost spiritual beings, created in God's image and wrapped in this transient bodily manifestation. The fact that we are living in a physical body distorts our perspective since it causes us to have such a strong attitude toward the physical world. But did you know that you, as a physical person, flicker millions of times each second in and out of time and space? It's not as obvious as you might think since it happens so quickly that our natural eyes can't tell the difference. Our being is a tangible manifestation of an energy flow, just like the bed you sleep in, the table you sit at, the chair you sit in - everything.

God's awareness of all things, in all of creation, at all times, holds this world together! Amazing! It's incredible what science is uncovering that changes our outlook on life. Yet, as Christians, we should be ecstatic that everything disclosed in these studies can be found in the Bible!

4:18 2 Corinthians While we look not at the things that can be seen, but at the things that cannot be seen: for what can be seen is transient, but what cannot be seen is eternal.

1:17 in Colossians And he is before everything, and everything depends on him.

Science has been uncovering the mysteries of the gospel and revealing them to us, especially in the last few decades, if we have an ear to hear. One such revelation is that humans are made up entirely of energy. As made human beings, we are considerably more bendable and have far more effect as energy than we are aware of.

We shall be effective to the extent that we are conscious of who we are in Christ and the dominion we have been given. Our knowledge of the interplay between ourselves and the environment around us, both physical and spiritual, has a significant impact on how we influence and are influenced by our surroundings. We must awaken to the totality of who we are meant to be while also being fully aware of the eternal and physical realms. As a soul wrapped in a physical body but not confined by its limitations, I have one foot in each realm! Our boundaries and frontiers are set by God alone, not by the physical environment. As we awaken to our position in Him, both in heavenly regions and on the earth, we must live in full awareness of this. While we are still in these mortal bodies on the earth, we are seated with Him in heavenly regions!

13:11 in Romans And that, understanding the time, this is the best time to wake up from your slumber: for our salvation is closer than we thought.

5:14 (Ephesians) As a result, he says, Awake, ye who slumber, and awake from the dead, and Christ will give thee light.

Both of these lines are about waking up from a dullness of mind and spirit so that we don't fall into the day's complacency, whether it's sin or unbelief. We can no longer afford to live our days, hours, and moments on autopilot; instead, we must become acutely aware of each and every present moment. We only have the present moment. What happened in the past is gone, and what will happen in the future hasn't happened yet, at least in our time and space realm. But we have limitless opportunities in every moment for how our lives can change, how our mindsets can evolve, and how our awareness can grow stronger, influencing not only ourselves, but the world around us.

2 Corinthians 5:16, 17 is a passage from the book of 2 Corinthians. As a result, we will no longer know anyone in the flesh: yea, though we have known Christ in the flesh, we will no longer know him. As a

result, everybody who believes in Christ is a new creature: old things have passed away, and all things have become new.

Regrettably, we continue to believe in the old ways. We still think that the constraints imposed on man between the fall and the resurrection of Christ govern us! Let this not be the case anymore! We have no concept what a magnificent creation we are in Christ and have been living in the deafening monotony of what has gone before - the old man's way! When words are spoken into our ears, they are nothing more than vibrations to which we have given meaning. The vibrations of air molecules send a signal to the inner ear, which then sends a message to the auditory region of our brain, where it is transmitted and has an impact on our entire being. We have no knowledge of what is being said if it is a language we don't comprehend, and our bodies don't respond or become aware of what has been transmitted if it is a language we don't understand. If it is in a language we recognize, on the other hand, we identify the sound and it effects us in either a positive or bad way, depending on the message. It can create a cellular reaction as if you had just injected a chemical-based substance into your body! That's how much our emotional and spiritual reactions to things may affect our bodies, our entire selves. Medicine is only now beginning to grasp the truth of how the body, mind, and soul are intertwined. That is how God intended for us to engage with one another and our environment. That is why, throughout the Bible, Christ encourages us to focus on the positive, on "whatever things are pure." Everything we come across has an effect on us. Any two particles that have ever collided are forever linked. Science is now discovering how (one) we are in Christ, who is the source of all things!

Philippians 4:7–8, Philippians Through Christ Jesus, the peace of God, which surpasses all understanding, will guard your hearts and minds. Finally, brethren, whatever things are true, whatever things are honest, whatever things are just, whatever things are pure, whatever things are lovely, whatever things are worthy of praise, consider these things.

Being conscious of the positive aspects of ourselves and those around us at all times of the day and night could drastically alter our lives. That is why, throughout the Bible, He encourages us to cultivate a grateful heart so that we can live in a state of abiding love. Being aware of the flow of God in us at all times - in this present now - so that we are always aware of our oneness with Him would allow us to see the world in a different light. I'm wondering whether this is why Paul tells us to pray without stop. Maybe that's why he found it so advantageous to pray in tongues all the time, to the point that he declared, "I pray in tongues more than ALL of you!" It brought him to a position where he was acutely aware of his oneness with God.

Yes, our own understanding of God's goodness in these days will go a great way toward helping us get through some difficult situations. We would do well to be awakened to the reality of the Spirit realm and the spiritual truths found in scripture, which may overcome what we see and don't see with our natural eyes. As we wash God's perspective on things over our brains and hearts, we put on the whole armor of God.

Does this imply that there aren't any issues?

No, but we walk through them with "grace grace" on our lips and the same acute awareness of God's love and goodness at all times as Paul had, allowing miracles to flow through him.

4:6, 7 (Zechariah) Then he spoke to me, saying, This is the word of the LORD to Zerubbabel, saying, Not by might, nor by power, but by my spirit, says the LORD of hosts. O mighty mountain, who are you? You shall become a plain before Zerubbabel, and he shall bring forth the headstone of it with shoutings and crying, Grace, grace unto it.

It's time to refocus our attention on things that have eternal value, so that we might be the ones to offer healing and deliverance to the people in this hour. We've all heard that the darkness will grow darker and the light will grow brighter, but we can't assume that we'll be able to enjoy this light unless we've first looked into it. As we gaze upon Him, we are transformed. As we "focus our thoughts on things above," we must develop our spirit man in order to gain strength and mental clarity.

17:15 (Psalms) As for me, I will see thy face in righteousness, and I will be satisfied with thy resemblance when I awake.

Being eternally present with Him means being conscious that He is in us and we are in Him at all times. We will notice changes in ourselves and the environment around us as a result of that present consciousness, that state of oneness. We were created in the image of the One Who was, is, and will be!

Churches have morphed into mini-seminaries, with many holding multiple teaching sessions every week. When truth has nowhere to go, rot sets in. We become skilled listeners, but we are mislead if our listening does not proceed to the point of our doing. Deception does not have to be based on dishonesty or open wickedness that is artfully disguised as respectability. Teaching that isn't grounded on discipleship has no place in the lives of people. The goal of leadership and ministry is to develop a group of people who are competent of carrying out the task. Our institutions and schools have developed a leadership that is capable of accomplishing anything. When truth and practice are not integrated, error occurs. Many church meetings are organized to carry out the goals that the students achieved while attending Bible college. Instead of generating disciples to fulfill the ministry's work, preaching well-prepared sermons has become the aim. Some churches have neglected other important areas of life in the Kingdom as a result of our unadulterated passion for Scripture and conveying truth. Body ministry is a foundational biblical notion that is often overlooked. We will never grow up into all things in God if all we are is pew food for the teaching and preaching of a small number of "qualified" people.

The following are the questions that leaders must ask. What is it, and why is it important? What exactly are we up to, and why are we up to it? Is it possible for our church's structure, culture, and model to be used to bring individuals into a deeper experience of God, the practice of truth, and pathways of service and supernatural expression?

The growth of worship and love for God is a key question. "Are we devoting enough attention to the biblical and practical implications of developing new forms of adoration, devotion, and worship?" Worship must evolve over time as devotion develops.

Do we actually teach people how to worship through song, dance, and art? Are there any devotional courses that help people develop their personal quiet times with God? Is our congregation aware of the distinction between personal worship, in which we all sing together, and corporate worship, in which we intentionally engage in a communal and focused action in order to minister to God?

We don't do a good job of reconciling reality with experience and practice. We have placed a premium on precise doctrine and a thorough comprehension of Scripture, but we have overlooked the role of experience in the maturation of mature believers. The biblical orthodoxy has devolved into a religious wasteland. We defend the truth to the point of death, which is wonderful, but we do not fully live it out. Our greatest strength has turned into our most revealing flaw. Our connection with God has no place to go if we don't have any experience. It's like knowing everything there is to know about romantic love relationships but never marrying. All of your knowledge is contained in a book of study notes. The relationship's experience allows us to write the truth on the tables of our hearts, which is a poetic manner of expressing experience.

I'm fascinated by both what God doesn't say and what He does say in our lives. Structure, organization, form, and substance appeal to us as humans. We desire specific details because we want to know what God is up to and where He is leading us. Abraham, on the other hand, had to go without knowing where he was heading.

11:8 in Hebrews By faith, Abraham obeyed when he was summoned to go out into a land that he would later inherit, and he went out, not knowing where he was going.

God sometimes withholds detailed vision in order for us to walk by faith. He'll give us broad guidelines rather than particular goals. Like prophecy, vision is something we see in part and know in part. God only gives us enough to glimpse the next step or a few of phases in broad terms. We gain additional knowledge and direction when we achieve those objectives.

When it comes to meetings, God is a little hazy. He actually only says two things.

10:25 in Hebrews Not neglecting the assembling of ourselves together, as some would have us do, but exhorting one another, and all the more as the day approaches.

14:26-33 in 1 Corinthians So, how are things doing, brethren? Every one of you has a psalm, a theology, a tongue, a revelation, and an interpretation when you gather together. Let everything be done for the sake of edification. If somebody speaks in an unknown tongue, let it be between two or three people, and that only if necessary; and let one interpret. If there is no interpreter available, he should remain silent in the church and speak only to himself and to God. Allow two or three prophets to speak, and the other to judge. Let the first keep his peace if something is revealed to another who sits nearby. For each of you may prophesy one by one, so that all may learn and be consoled. The prophets' spirits are also susceptible to the prophets. Because, like in all churches of the saints, God is not the author of turmoil, but of peace.

This section does not provide specific instructions on how to conduct meetings. Most church meetings would be unbiblical if it did! It discusses the possibilities and what might occur. Surprisingly, it all revolves around supernatural utterance, which is unlikely to apply to many churches. Is it possible that our churches are unbiblical because they lack divine utterance? It's only a query. There is no mention of form or organization in this paragraph. There is no indication of when to sing, teach, pray, or do anything else. It only refers to the degree of creativity and spontaneity that arise from our relationship with the Holy Spirit. I'm not suggesting that every meeting should be open, creative, and completely unscripted.

It's impossible for every meeting to be the same. We are not putting God or them first by attempting to shoehorn them into a stereotypical meeting. Meetings should be planned with goals in mind. Let us respond appropriately if our goal is to teach others how to worship God collectively. Allow for freedom of movement and expression in a workshop setting by removing the seats (if possible!). Let us hold a seminar-like session in whichever format is appropriate for interactive learning if our goal is training. If we want members to be able to freely share what they believe the Holy Spirit is saying, we need to set up shop accordingly.

The majority of Sunday services are tediously familiar. In certain establishments, such as McDonalds, the order of service is announced prior to the gathering. Perhaps the only true difference between certain churches and McDonald's is that a fast food restaurant is less expensive, has a nicer ambience, we can get in and out quickly, and we're probably better fed! Stereotyped believers result from stereotypical services. God's creativity is limitless. Any one-dimensional state is challenged by his nature. If they're for God, we should structure them according to His wishes, keeping in mind His creative nature. If they're for people, then let's organize the meeting around the goal we've set. If we organize our meetings according to a specific formula because that is how we have always done it, we have completely missed the purpose and have become unbiblical in the process. If the stereotype is simply our most efficient way of managing people, time, and resources, then we need to reassess what church is all about.

God can be hazy about how church works at times, but he wants us to gain sensitivity as we follow the Spirit's lead. The Bible frequently refers to duty, operation, and purpose without mentioning specific shapes, patterns, or models. The reason for this is that the format in which we operate will vary frequently, although the task and operation will likely remain consistent. The form is the wineskin, which must be lubricated on the outside to keep its supple shape and prevent fresh wine from cracking it open. Similarly, the church's form and shape must be altered on a regular basis to keep up with the continuing nature of God's work.

For the sake of stability, safety, and security, humans will always set things in stone. While this is admirable, it actually works against us. Only God and one another provide us with protection. Relationships of grace and love, not corporate structure, provide security. If God wants to continue to work with us in strength and purpose, we must overthrow our concrete structure. It's a pity that the Lord has to set in action a whole chain of circumstances simply to get into our fortifications! People misinterpret this as battle and resist it, resulting in church divisions. The Holy Spirit is never the one who splits the church. The wineskin is frequently dry and cracked, unable to handle the new item that God wishes to bring. We try to find a middle ground, but it's like mending an old garment with new fabric; it won't work!

Many people oppose the change that God intends to bring when our safety and security in the shape of what we have made is threatened. Even when the Bible does define a model or a pattern, it does so in a non-descriptive manner. In terms of long-term identification, the model will be constrained. Models do not last for years and are continually changing. To take into consideration what is going on with people, the modifications may be slight. Our mission is to alter people and turn them into the likeness of Jesus. We must modify the model and form we build around them in order for that shift to be complete. The wineskin must evolve as the people change. If people change but the church's form and structure do not, we shall have severe problems with the Holy Spirit. Leaders who refuse to change are doomed to be replaced.

People should follow Paul in the same way that he followed Christ, according to the apostle Paul. God is ambiguous about patterns, models, church operations, and form and structure because He understands that a one-dimensional Church would be impossible to exist due to the diversity of cultures. They would be imprisoned and killed because of their faith, as they are in many nations today. In many countries, it is illegal for Christians to meet in public. Is this enough to rule them out as unbiblical? Because the main premise we're working with is being guided by the Spirit, the Bible is unclear about shape and structure.

As people react to the Lord and mature in their faith, churches will alter. The evolving nature of church is also influenced by cultural constraints. Whether that culture is the result of different national characteristics or simply the difference between youth and the elderly; street people and upper middle class society; the intelligent or the illiterate, it will all have an impact on how we operate as a church.

One of the most difficult challenges we face in establishing a church is changing the stereotypes that certain groups of people have created. If we are more devoted to our structure than to the Lord, we have created an idol out of what we have created. It will have to come down because God will not allow it. The Holy Spirit will overthrow anything that inhibits God from moving among His people. This occurs when God displays to His bride all that He desires to do and be through willing individuals. Unfortunately, these individuals are branded as disruptive, unteachable, and rebellious. To be fair, some of them couldn't control their rage, but that doesn't make them rebels.

The stresses of growth, creativity, maturation, and the generation of anointed persons who can battle will be understood by the fivefold ministries of apostle, prophet, pastor, teacher, and evangelist. Each will participate in their own manner to the construction of the prototype of a new church that will have to live on the battlefield. Each one has a razor-sharp edge that is meant to be aggressive, arousing, and provocative. Apostles despise mediocrity in all of its forms. They'll go after phony ministries, phony reasons, and phony lifestyles.

Paul was a tireless advocate for moral purity, interpersonal harmony, and doctrinal clarity. In such locations, he assaulted and condemned individuals who disobeyed God. Injustice, unethical behavior, repressive governments, and stereotypical impediments to what the Lord wishes to do are all attacked by prophets. They serve as a catalyst for life's sanctity and loving relationships. When I enter into my Apostleship, I get a lot of criticism. The apostles compel the Church to listen to God's current word and make all necessary adjustments. Teachers are assigned to encourage the union of truth and discipleship, as well as knowledge and experience. They go after unbelief and stupidity. They understand that when the full truth is revealed, it will result in a crisis. Anyone who does not live a life that is consistent with Scripture will clash with the Holy Spirit.

Teachers understand that Spirit-induced crises necessitates the formation of mature responses via repentance and obedience. As a result, all truth must be pursued. If it isn't, condemnation will follow because the enemy will fill the void if there isn't a repentant response.

Pastors will have a role in this transformation, collaborating with teachers to develop a positive belief system that can permanently alter our behavior. When dealing with tensions, conflicts, acts of rebellion, and people's historical baggage, pastors practice the art of loving confrontation.

As they engage a sin-sick society with the gospel, evangelists must stand up against worldly value systems and false philosophies. The gospel message is disputed, controversial, and confrontational, yet it is pervaded by revelations of a loving God's generosity, kindness, and mercy, who paid the price for us to live in His presence for all eternity.

I hope we can grasp the process and the crisis that frequently precedes it. The conclusions we reach regarding our own work will have a significant impact on our growth and future

16

~

Imaginative Ideas

Every believer possesses the power to have creative thoughts. If you pay attention to what I'm saying in this chapter, it will change your life. Here's a more in-depth look at the mind, particularly the creative potential of thoughts.

2 Corinthians 12:2 And do not be conformed to this world, but be changed by the renewing of your mind, so that you may demonstrate what is God's good, acceptable, and perfect will.

When our minds are refreshed, our entire life will be transformed and metamorphosed. This will enable us to soar and not be bound by the world's norms of living and being; we will be completely capable of demonstrating God's good, acceptable, and perfect will.

When we encounter different words, pictures, situations, etc., our minds are programmed and set to respond in a certain way or project a certain impression. They have preconceived notions and attitudes about church based on previous experiences: a church they visited as a child, a religious fanatic they saw on television, or the zealous preacher on the car radio.

That attitude is about to change and be rejuvenated. The Bride of Christ is ready to transform into a celestial creature. Spiritual strongholds that prevent us from soaring are ungodly and worldly thoughts. The metamorphosis that occurs as a result of the pressure and isolation in the cocoon breaks these bonds.

The constrictions and pressures that the Lord allows to come upon us in the cocoon release us. The bonds of self-dependence are dissolved as we rely more and more on the Holy Spirit, who strengthens us in our inner being so that we can reach greater heights. Those who wish to escape these tests will be consigned to the earth as worms. We have the option of moving with the Spirit's current and letting the hardships of this age work for us, or we can continue wading through the shallow water and never reach our objective, which is only reached after the rapids. Matthew 10:39 quotes Jesus. He who finds his life will lose it, whereas he who loses it for my cause will find it.

The hardships and tribulations of this age, according to Paul, are nothing in comparison to the glory that will be revealed to us, in us, and through us.

8:18 in Romans Because I believe that our current hardships are insignificant in comparison to the brilliance that will be revealed in us.

Unfortunately, many leaders have repressed and kept the Church in its infancy due to a lack of maturity; they are in danger of losing everything. This transformation is required. Attempting to save someone from it is harmful to him. To develop blood flow into its extremities, the chick needs to struggle to break out of the egg. If not, the baby has a good likelihood of dying soon after birth. Walking in the fullness of life necessitates the struggle for life.

Humans, like God, have a creative ability that can be used to recreate the world around us using the mind.

139:14 Psalms I will praise thee because I am fearfully and wonderfully made; marvellous are thy works, as my soul knows.

We were made in God's image and likeness. Humankind possesses the same creative nature as God. The most excellent way to release creative authority is through love. There is still a fuller and more abundant way to minister the mind, heart, and power of God in the earth, even with all that has been given to humanity in terms of Holy Spirit gifts and the ability to cooperate with the Spirit of God in the anointing.

12:31 in 1 Corinthians But covet the best gifts with all your heart, and yet I will show you a better way.

13:9-13 in 1 Corinthians We only know in part and can only fore-tell in part. When that which is perfect comes, however, that which is imperfect will be done away with. When I was a youngster, I spoke, understood, and thought like a child; nevertheless, when I grew up, I put away childish things. Because we see through a glass, dimly now, but face to face later: now I know in part, but afterwards I will know even as I am known. And now these three remain: faith, hope, and charity; but the greatest of them is charity.

Many people interpret the phrase "when the perfect comes" to refer to the second coming of Christ. The phrase, on the other hand, is about love. The entire chapter is dedicated to love and how it may enhance our lives. Paul is referring to a new benchmark, a new level. He claims that while we should truly pursue the highest gifts and graces, there is still a better route, which he calls the way of love.

5:6 (Galatians) For neither circumcision nor uncircumcision avail anything in Jesus Christ, but faith working through love.

Looking through a darkly tinted window will be obsolete when that which is flawless arrives. From one level to the next, we will come to this perfection of love more totally, truly, and intimately.

It is critical that we remember that thoughts are seeds. Thoughts have life and will replicate, which simply implies that everything reproduces in the same way.

1:11, 12 Galatians But I assure you, friends, that the gospel that

I taught is not a man-centered gospel. For I did not receive it from a man, nor was I taught it, but by Jesus Christ's revelation.

This law of creation has an ongoing impact on us since it forms our future and decides our present. Our circumstances are still being shaped by this law. Stop blaming everyone and their brother, including the devil, for our current predicament and take responsibility for what is developing in our life. This creation law is unchangeable and irreversible. We plant trees and gardens, and they multiply in the same way that they were planted. The garden of our hearts is the fertile soil where we unwittingly sow the majority of seeds. What you plant there will grow and reproduce. Thoughts are nothing more than seeds. The heat that drives the seed to spin into life is passion and deep desire. Babies are conceived out of love. Inner desire, in the same way, gives life to the seeds in our hearts.

23:7 (Proverbs) For he is as he thinks in his heart: Eat and drink, he says, but his heart is not with thee.

This suggests that a person will become what he believes and thinks in his heart. What he thinks will come to pass in his life.

Matthew 7:1 If you don't judge, you won't be judged. For with what judgment you judge, you will be judged, and with what measure you mete, you will be measured back.

The seed of judgment sown will bear fruit in the form of a tree of judgment. Because of this law, we must live every moment as we wish the future to be in thought and action. The human mind is one of the most powerful forces on the planet.

11:23 (Mark) For verily I say unto you, whosoever shall say to this mountain, "Be removed and cast into the sea," and shall not doubt in his heart, but believe that those things which he saith shall come to pass, he shall have whatever he saith.

Jesus isn't using metaphors here. He's speaking figuratively. For this to work, you don't even have to be a Christian. This idea alone has resulted in a large number of persons unlawfully showing supernatural feats and talents. Keep in mind that the human mind is a tremendous earthly force; this universal rule cannot be altered.

11:24 (Mark) As a result, I say to you, whatever it is that you wish, believe that you will receive it when you pray, and you will.

Jesus is saying that if you believe, have faith, and desire what you're asking for, you'll get it. Our ideas aren't fleeting, unimportant wisps; they're desire seeds that produce and design the direction of our present and future lives. How are thoughts sown if they are seeds? A supernatural power or energy is released when an idea firmly unites with emotion. It releases the power of life and light if you hold your thoughts until they are connected to your emotions, feelings, and desires. Matthew 18:19 is a good example of this principle. Again, I say to you, that if two of you agree on earth as to anything they ask for, it will be done for them by my Father who is in heaven.

It will be completed when your emotions and your mind are in sync. This is the power of collective bargaining. It is effective against both divine and evil concepts. When this seed of thinking is ignited by emotion, it will literally generate an atmosphere of love and joy in your home. Any thoughts that connect with our emotions become a powerful force that shapes the environment around us.

For years, the Church has preached that emotions are unimportant. I believe that your emotions, as well as your thinking life, constitute your creative side. Everything depends on your emotions to happen. Jesus was moved by compassion and performed miracles as a result.

Matthew 20:34 So Jesus felt sympathy for them and touched their eyes, and their eyes were immediately opened, and they followed him.

Mark 1:41 And Jesus, moved by compassion, stretched out his hand and touched him, saying, "I will; be clean."

Compassion brings about miracles, even the resurrection of the dead.

7:11-17 The next day, he traveled into a city called Nain,

accompanied by many of his disciples and a large number of people. When he got close to the city gate, he saw a dead guy being taken out, his mother's only son, and she was a widow, and many others from the city were with her. When the Lord saw her, he was moved by compassion and said to her, "Do not weep." And he came up to the bier and touched it, and those who bore him remained still. And he said to him, "Young man," he said, "I say unto thee, Arise." And the dead man awoke and began to speak. And he handed him over to his mother. All were terrified, and they praised God, saying, "A great prophet has arisen among us," and "God has visited his people." And word of him spread across all of Judaea, as well as throughout the surrounding country.

The anointing's power and glory are released through the channel of human affection.

6:12 in 2 Corinthians You are not restless in us, but restless in your own intestines.

What we do must be felt. Desire plants a seed and a power is released when our mind combines with our feelings.

1:15 James Then, after lust has conceived, it gives birth to sin, and sin, when completed, gives birth to death.

We must be cautious about what we think! We make a spiritual offering at the door of our minds every time we think, energizing and powering that thought. When the concept and the feeling come together, an evil desire is born. This creates a creative power link of agreement, which results in death. Brings forth is the same as a plant that is generated from a seed and signifies to breed or create. When I reflect on the Word and revelation begins to come, my entire being appears to be flooded with light, not just light, but with God's peaceful serenity and vitality. The revelation from God's intellect travels through my emotions and creates space for seed to be planted and grow in my spirit man. Revelation is more than just a concept; it's also an emotion that buries life deep within us. The seeds have been planted, and conception has occurred. The revelation will give birth in our lives if it is watered. A man will become what he thinks.

This new generation of Glory will progress in their awareness of how to use the creative potential of the imagination to create wonders. They will bring God's intentions and plans to fruition on the planet, wielding incredible power over natural elements. The creative force of the imagination is a Kingdom reality created by God to manifest in the natural what is seen in the spirit. It is not a New Age or occult idea. Curses that materialize from unholy allegiances can be used by the evil world of the occult to bring disaster to the natural world. However, God has given us the ability to use our imaginations to fall under the influence of the Holy Spirit and bring life, freedom, and destiny into our lives. Unfortunately, we've been taught that everything that involves using our imagination is New Age and is utilized to further the dark kingdom's agenda. In reality, New Agers and the occult have taken something really valuable from God's saints and distorted it to the point where we are terrified to approach it. It's past time for us to reclaim our ability to imagine. It's past time for us to start wreaking havoc on the reign of darkness with what God has given us!

We must picture ourselves as we wish to be in God. In fact, we must recognize ourselves as we truly are in Christ in order for it to become a reality in our lives. The imagination is a creative tool that takes what is hidden in the invisible realm into the physical sphere. We can use our imaginations to change the world around us for the better or for the worst. You can't walk in something until you've walked in it yourself. "Visualizing is New Age," you remark. Since the moment you were born, you've been visualizing. You're visualizing every time you think about anything, every time you daydream. It's a natural element of the creative process.

Throughout history, there have been a handful of persons who have broken through simple spiritual notions into upper Kingdom realities. They grasped the true meaning of Kingdom laws and began to put them into practice. Only a few people have reached a degree in God where they are capable of overcoming any earthly obstacle, including death. It's not just Enoch. It's simple to blame the devil and others for our current circumstances, but our current circumstances are a direct outcome of where our hearts are set in thought.

5:28 in Matthew But I say to you, whoever looks at a woman in order to lust for her has already committed adultery with her in his heart.

Everyone who looks with his eyes and thinks with his mind has already committed and hatched adultery in his heart. The imagination and the mind are the same thing. It's as if you've already completed the task.

There is life and brightness in every particle. God breathed the universe into existence with His imagination. The newly generated atoms were all spinning in unison, each in accordance with their own frequency, their own constructed order. When Adam, however, fell from God's Glory, the result was so dramatic that it tipped the world's axis. The earth wasn't the only thing that shifted; each atom was thrown out of sync with its initial rotation. Even at the subatomic level, everything was affected. When this happened, Satan had a free hand to corrupt and change things genetically. The good news is that everything in the universe was designed to respond to love. If we are radiating love, even the tiniest particle may sense it and respond to it. Atoms were created out of love, and as a result, they feel and respond to love. Animals, trees, and the rest of nature are all aware of it. Because they recognize your sonship and realize that you have reign over the planet, atoms will cooperate and speak in your favor. What you emit leaves a trail and has an impact on everyone and everything around you. If you arrive home with a sour attitude, your cat or dog will be the first to notice it before you even open your mouth. Because it is sensitive to emotion, Creation knows. All of creation eagerly awaits the day when God's children fully comprehend their sonship.

We have the capacity and authority to set Creation free from the bonds of decay, corruption, sin, and death that entered the earth with the Fall.

(Rom. 8:19-21) Because the creature's genuine expectation is for the manifestation of God's sons. Because the creature was subjected to vanity, not willingly, but because of him who had subjected it in hope, Because the creature will be set free from the bonds of corruption and enter the magnificent liberty of God's offspring.

13:10 in 1 Corinthians When that which is perfect comes, however, that which is imperfect will be done away with.

All of creation responds to a higher and more perfect form of love. The curse will be lifted and creation will experience freedom through love. Love brings signs, wonders, and miracles; all we have to do is keep doubt at bay.

9:23 in Mark If thou canst believe, all things are possible for him who believeth, Jesus stated.

If you don't believe, I feel it's safe to say that not much is possible. When we ask God for something, James says we should do so with trust and not with doubt in our hearts.

1:6 James But let him ask in faith, without hesitation. He who wavereth is like a wave of the sea that is thrown by the wind.

He goes on to clarify what we should expect from the Lord if we do have any doubts in our hearts.

James 1:7–8 For such individual must not believe that he will get anything from the Lord. In every way, a man who has two minds is unstable.

Doubt leads to unbelief, and unbelief is a powerful evil force that separates us from God's promises. Unbelief is a spirit that wears a black, demonic hood of deception and blindness. This spirit must be dealt with violently. We shouldn't have a single doubt in our minds.

Mark 1:15 records Jesus' words. And said, "The time has come for the kingdom of God to be established; repent, and believe the gospel."

Do you see what I mean? Doubt and disbelief are conquered through repenting and turning to the Lord, altering our thinking, and finally believing. This can sometimes necessitate a bold leap of faith in the right direction and a firm commitment to believe. To put our thoughts and imaginations in faith until they connect with our sentiments and emotions, we must learn to keep our concentration on the Lord. When we do this on a regular basis, heavenly seeds are sown, and faith grows, flourishes, and comes alive. We must learn to see ourselves in light of these considerations. Begin to visualize yourself walking in your destiny and aligning yourself with God's Kingdom. It is going to happen. This is how things are. In the beginning, God accomplished it this way: He thought it, saw it, and spoke it into reality. Remember:

23:7 (Proverbs) For he is as he thinks in his heart: Eat and drink, he says, but his heart is not with thee.

We have the option of believing and receiving or doubting and not receiving.

There are a lot of things about God that intrigue me, but none of them compare to the mystery of our identity in Christ. Just thinking about how we were made from the same piece of fabric as God makes my heart race with excitement. When I consider what it would be like to be living in eternity before I was born or before the worlds were created, it gets me curious about the truth of that life. I'm curious as to what it's like and what's going on. The truth is that you are a spirit. Your spirit originated in Heaven and has existed for a long time. Your spirit remembers what it was like to live in Heaven.

When your spirit was born into your body, it got entwined with your soul, and memories began to fade and finally vanish. Jesus was a Spirit before he was born on our planet. He existed within the Father's womb. He arrived on the planet as a Spirit and lived in a physical form with a soul.

1:8 John No one has ever seen God; he has been declared by the only begotten Son, who is in the bosom of the Father.

Jesus is still a man, body, soul, and spirit. Since He came from the dead, He now has a resurrected body. Yes, we are spirits, but God also created a soul and a body for us. In Christ, we are new creations.

5:17 in 2 Corinthians As a result, everybody who believes in Christ is a new creature: old things have passed away, and all things have become new.

We are spiritual creatures, but we are also human beings. All of our spirits, souls, and bodies must align with the Kingdom of God, but this can only happen through the spirit.

5:23 in 1 Thessalonians And may the God of peace purify you completely; and may God keep your whole spirit, soul, and body blameless until the return of our Lord Jesus Christ.

It's critical that our spirit, soul, and body come together as one so that we can interact with both the spiritual and physical realms. Heaven began as a spiritual realm. But then, in the Garden of Eden, God created the earth and brought Heaven into it. He manifested Heaven in the physical realm. Christ came into your spirit when you were born again, and in that seed is the entirety of the Godhead: Father, Son, and Holy Spirit. You are bursting at the seams with all of eternity's past, present, and future.

1 2 John 20 You, on the other hand, have an unction from the Holy One and know everything.

Everything that has happened in the past, is happening now, and will happen in the future has already been written on the fabric of your spirit person. When you unite with the Holy Spirit, you gain access to all knowledge.

While serving, I often find myself seeing things via the impact of my intellect in the spirit. When ministering in the Holy Spirit, I've realized that I'm under the power of the supernatural, and that what comes into my thoughts is from Heaven. I've also discovered that by speaking in the natural about what I'm seeing in the spirit, I'm laying the groundwork for those things to manifest in the natural. The spirit realm's actuality is all around us. The Holy Spirit will sometimes just give you a hunch or a fleeting impression. What occurs if you follow Him, though, will astonish you. Because you followed the tiniest push from the Holy Spirit, some of the most astounding miracles in your life will occur.

God promised Abraham's offspring would be like the stars when he was old. How did Abraham manage to be the father of two powerful nations? God instructed him to gaze into the heavens and gaze at the stars. Abraham raised his eyes to the sky and gazed as though he believed. When he envisioned the situation as a reality, it became possible. He saw his family as he gazed at the skies. God wants us to take an active role in realizing our potential. God makes a promise, but we don't look up; we don't visualize; we don't view the impossible circumstance with faith-filled eyes. The impossible becomes possible when we employ our imaginations in accordance with God's promises. God refers to things that do not yet exist as though they do. God already perceived the earth as having shape and substance when it was formless and emptiness, and merely summoned it forth.

4:13 in 2 Corinthians We, having the same faith spirit, believe, and so speak; we, too, believe, and thus speak; if we picture ourselves sick, broken, and poor, that is exactly what will be born in our life. Things will manifest in our lives if we begin to imagine ourselves as God's blessings and start calling things that aren't as if they are. We must believe and speak regardless of our ethnicity, gender, socioeconomic background, or familial circumstances. Let us follow Abraham's example and gaze up at the stars.

Matthew 8:5-13 When Jesus arrived in Capernaum, a centurion approached him, pleading with him, saying, Lord, my servant is sick of the palsy at home, afflicted greatly. And Jesus says to him, "Come, and I will heal him." The centurion replied, "Lord, I am not worthy for thee to enter my house; but pronounce only the word, and my servant shall be healed." For I am a commander with soldiers under me, and I tell this man, "Go," and he goes; and I tell another, "Come," and he comes; and I tell my servant, "Do this," and he does it. When Jesus heard it, he was taken aback and told the crowd, "Truly, I say unto you, I have not found such great faith, no, not in Israel." And I tell to you, many will come from the east and west to sit with Abraham, Isaac, and Jacob in the heavenly kingdom. The children of the kingdom, on the other hand, will be sent out into the outer darkness, where they will wail and gnash their teeth. And Jesus said to the centurion, "Go your way," and "as you have believed, so shall it be done to you." His servant was also healed at the same time.

Our imaginations, I feel, are a component of humanity's creative essence. Everything God created previously existed in His mind and heart before He spoke it into existence. Everything a person creates begins in his head, in his imagination. We understand that faith is a matter of the heart as well as the mind. God is asking us to trust Him when He wants us to have faith in Him. It's all about the heart when it comes to trust. True faith, on the other hand, does not stay in the heart; it begins in the heart and spreads to the rest of the person, including the mind, imagination, and, finally, every action and speech.

We see Jesus promising to come to the centurion's servant and heal him in the narrative of the centurion's faith. Although Jesus was quite content to go the extra mile, the centurion was convinced that his servant would be healed if only Jesus spoke the word. The centurion's faith was based on what he heard. He had his mind made up and was completely convinced in the authority of the spoken word because he was a guy of authority, a man of the spoken word. It's in the way you think, envision, and believe that your religion is founded.

"As you imagine, it will be done unto you," you could say, because imagination fosters faith and belief. The account of the woman with a blood issue in the Bible is another illustration of this.

Mark 5:27, 28 When she heard about Jesus, she went behind the press and touched his garment. She claimed that if she could only touch his garments, she would be healed.

3:1, 2 Colossians If you have been raised with Christ, seek those things that are above, where Christ sits at God's right side. Set your affection on things that are above you, not on things that are below you.

We shall experience breakthrough as we fix our gaze on Jesus and continue to seek the things above with our minds and imaginations. We will literally perceive the eternal realm. Everything will change when we catch a sight of Jesus. We must utilize our imaginations to reconstruct our entire thinking lives during this process. We must learn to submit everything of our thoughts to Christ's obedience and to fix our affections on things above.

10:5 in 2 Corinthians We will begin to see ourselves and everyone around us through the eyes of Christ, casting down imaginations and every high thing that exalts itself against the knowledge of God, and bringing every idea into captivity to the obedience of Christ. We shall begin to see our future glory and destiny. Only then will we be able to bring it into the present day.

1 Thessalonians 1:17, 18 That the Father of Glory, the God of our Lord Jesus Christ, may give you the spirit of wisdom and revelation in the knowledge of him, the eyes of your understanding being enlightened, that ye may know what is the hope of his calling, and what the riches of the glory of his inheritance in the saints,

When we stare into the everlasting realm with comprehending eyes, we are gazing into the true realm. God can communicate with us via our imagination, the devil can communicate with us through our imagination, and we can communicate with ourselves through our imagination. It is coming from us if we are imagining anything from our own minds. Outside-of-us ideas, on the other hand, come from one of two places: God or the devil. We may be imagining something from ourselves when, out of nowhere, we receive something from God or the devil. What was the source of that? You might believe that I wasn't even considering it! You were open to the spirit realm because you were using your imagination. Because our imaginations are the gateway and link that connects the spiritual and natural worlds, the spirit realm enjoys imprinting sights and thoughts into our minds. If a person receives ungodly pictures on a regular basis, they may believe it is all in their head. In reality, they are possessed by a demonic spirit who has taken up residence in their minds. That demonic entity is the imagination's gatekeeper, watching over what enters and exits. As one with the Holy Spirit, our spirit should be the guardian of our ideas. This is why it's so important to wash our minds with pure water so that those mental and imaginative strongholds can be broken and replaced.

When we find our minds wandering at random and leading us into perversity, it's a sign that we have strongholds in our minds and need deliverance. It's as simple as starving those strongholds and mindsets and letting the powerful blood of Jesus Christ wash over us to bring us freedom. We must watch what enters our eye-gates and ear-gates since we are the caretakers of our minds. It was either you or someone else who started daydreaming. The spirit world is continually trying to reach out to us. In the Bible, the great majority of God's contact with mankind took the form of visions and dreams. Remember that a person becomes what he thinks in his heart. Someone other than us has access to our thinking. Who is it, exactly? Acquire the ability to observe things for yourself. Accept what is good and reject what is bad. To distinguish the voice of God from all the other sounds, train your mind and spiritual senses. If you want to walk with God, you must first learn to walk with Him in your imagination, with your understanding's eyes enlightened so that you can understand God's things.

The imagination is a gift from God that should be used to bring the invisible into the visible realm. God intended for us to be thinking, imaginative, and visionary people who, via the sanctified imagination, can think and act like God.

4:17 in Romans (I have made thee a father of many nations, as it is written,) before him whom he believed, even God, who quickeneth the dead and calls those things which are not as if they were.

God has given us the ability to create in a variety of ways, not just through procreation or reproduction, but also aesthetically and visually. Like our heavenly Father, we are inventive and creative. Every tangible item in your immediate environment, whether it's a clock, a picture frame, or a coffee cup, has been designed with a certain bit of imagination and creativity. Every masterpiece that has ever been created began in the artist's mind.

It's critical that we see ourselves through God's eyes. We are Heaven's citizens. We must be transformed from normal to heavenly ways of thinking. Adam was the first living soul when God breathed the breath of life into him. God breathed all eternity into Adam when He breathed the breath of life. Adam's destiny, identity, citizenship, origin, imagination, and the Spirit of Wisdom and Understanding all came directly from God and into him from the infinity of eternities.

139:13-17 (Psalms) Because thou haste, I will praise thee because I am fearfully and wonderfully made; wondrous are thy works, as my soul knows. When I was fashioned in secret and strangely crafted in the lowest regions of the earth, my substance was not hidden from thee. Thine eyes saw my imperfect substance, and in thy book were written all of my members, which were continually fashioned, even though none of them existed at the time. O God, how valuable are thy thoughts to me! What a huge sum they make!

We are citizens of Heaven; we are not of this world. We are God's direct descendants. Isn't this indicative of our ability to return to the very place from which we came? We can use our imaginations to creatively bring what exists in the spirit into the natural world. For our families, friends, ministries, businesses, cities, states, and nations, we can release God's will. So, what's on your mind right now? What is your vision for the future?

Within your spirit, you have an immutable design and destiny from God. Most of the time, the desires in our hearts are the precise things that the Holy Spirit has sealed and arranged in us. We have the ability to birth and bring out our own futures. We'll agonize over it until it happens if we don't. When it's written all over us, many of us wonder what God's will is for our life.

In the Litchfield Revival, God gave me a new word. It's called visioning. This is when God's very thoughts consume your imagination. When I'm alone with the Lord in the Spirit, I visualize and shout out for the things I dream about: healing the masses, casting out devils with a word, and God confirming my words with mighty signs and wonders. I see God's glory sweeping across a football field-sized amphitheater, destroying it with Holy Spirit strength and fire. I envision God's strength enveloping an entire city, everyone being saved, and His bright Glory demonstrating miracles and healings in power! Then I watch as people enter the Lord's big congregation and testify to the amazing things God has done for them, one by one. Because I can see them, these things will happen in my lifetime! I've attended many of these Spirit-led events, and they're fantastic. God has given me the ability to bring these things to pass. They will occur, and I will play a role in aiding these divine acts of power.

29:18 (Proverbs) People perish where there is no vision; but he who keeps the law is joyful.

We shall begin to dry up on the vine and lose hope and confidence unless we imagine and give voice to these prophetic dreams and visions that come from the Holy One residing within us. If this occurs, we may finally settle for considerably less than God's most perfect will for us. For far too long, we've been told that we can't use our imaginations to engage God, but I'm here to tell you that you can. You are free to engage the third heavens and uncover truths and mysteries in the Kingdom of God under the guidance of the Holy Spirit.

If we want to have the same kinds of experiences as Ezekiel or Isaiah, we need to start meditating on their experiences in the third Heaven and begging the Lord for our own. We must spend time in the Holy Spirit's tremendous presence and utilize our imaginations to engage Heaven based on what John saw in Revelation and what Daniel, Ezekiel, and Isaiah observed. When we interact in this fashion, it's only a matter of time before we find ourselves in front of God's throne.

We shall be at a significant disadvantage unless we utilize our imaginations in a sanctified manner, as God intended, and reclaim the right to do so from the devil. God adores visionaries and dreamers who believe in His Word. We must reach out to God and allow Him to reach out to us. We must shake Heaven until we see the full manifestation of our heart's desires.

17

∽

Or you'll perish

We must rise, or we will die if we remain in our current state. This was a Word from the Lord to the Believers in the Waves of Revival. America is suffering from a leadership vacuum. This is true not only in government, but in almost every major center of power, including the church. We are warned in Isaiah chapters three through five that capricious, immature leaders are the beginning of God's wrath for a society that walks away from God and falls into the ultimate depravity of calling good evil and evil good, and honoring the honorable while dishonoring the dishonorable. That is an accurate depiction of the United States of America. It will take more than a presidential election to pull us out of this quagmire. We need a rebirth. We will not be able to endure much longer until another Great Awakening occurs.

The United States of America must prepare. This isn't to say the elections aren't significant. America, along with the rest of Western civilization, has been pushed to the brink of a potentially fatal cliff. The entire globe is poised to come crashing down on the rocks of financial insolvency, but financial issues are only the beginning of a far bigger catastrophe. The West has lost its spiritual and moral foundations, which are essential for our survival as a free people.

Money will not solve America's problems. A financial shift could give us more time, but without a change of mindset, we'll be back in the same spot in no time. America has fallen into almost every trap that the Founding Fathers predicted would bring the country to its knees. These warnings were specific and clear, and the consequences of continuing in our current path were accurately predicted. Congress and the White House have issued numerous warnings, but nothing has been done to alter the trajectory. More than knowing what needs to be done, leadership necessitates the confidence, resolve, and stamina to take the helm and sail the ship away from danger.

The heart of America is in God's gaze. Again, our issues aren't only financial; they're also character issues. The economy is simply a reflection of our current heart disease. We must assess what is being done and what the implications will be if we do not alter our course, but we must also assess why we are doing it.

In this hour, we must be cautious in our decisions. The entire planet is entering "decision valley." What will be our final decision? We may feel safer for a while if we follow the crowd, but we may also be putting ourselves in far more danger. "Hosanna!" cried the multitude as they welcomed Jesus into Jerusalem. "Crucify Him!" they cried out barely five days later, "Blessed is He who comes in the name of the Lord!" In such cases, the crowd's discernment has rarely been good. We all need a moral compass in our hearts to guide us regardless of whether others are following in our footsteps or not.

In the last three years, Americans have lost more freedoms than in the previous two centuries combined. Recent Obama Administration measures have been seen as a direct assault on the Catholic Church, but they are much more. They are a direct and brazen attack on the whole American church, as well as religious liberty. If the American church continues to slumber through what is happening to it, it will die very soon.

Where are the challengers to Herod, such as John the Baptist? This is a time for unwavering resolve and courage; if we are afraid, we will perish like John the Baptist. There are worse things than death, we must remember. It will be considerably worse to be a watchman who failed to sound the alarm or a shepherd who failed to protect those entrusted to them on the great Day of Judgment.

Revelations 21:8 is a passage from the book of Revelations. However, the fearful, unbelieving, and detestable, as well as murderers, whoremongers, sorcerers, idolaters, and all liars, will have their part in the lake of fire and brimstone, which is the second death.

Suffering now, even incarceration or death, will be preferable to suffering afterwards. Cowardice has no place in a true Christian's life. Those who sought to save their lives would lose them, but those who sought to lose their lives for His sake would find them, the Lord said.

Matthew 16:25 For whomever saves his life for my sake will lose it, and whoever loses his life for my cause will find it.

It is now our turn. This is the timepiece we're using. Will we demonstrate the courage required of true servants of the King?

John the Baptist had few prophetic experiences, but he was an uncompromising teacher of righteousness and justice. The entire nation was compelled to come out and listen to his message of repentance. To prepare the way for the Lord, repentance must be preached. It is the most critical message we can deliver at this time.

God determines righteousness and evil, not what political correctness thinks they are. Not long ago, America was a country that, perhaps more than any other, aligned itself with God's definition of righteousness and justice. As a result, we received what God promised to any nation that followed His instructions. Now we are beginning to see the consequences that He said would befall a nation that turned away from His ways, and it all started with a leadership vacuum.

The answer is to pursue repentance, which will lead us back to God's favor, and then He will rise up good leaders as a result.

7:14 in 2 Chronicles If my people, who are called by my name, humble themselves, pray, seek my face, and repent of their wicked ways, then I will hear from heaven, forgive their sin, and heal their land.

To heal a land, the Lord wants four things: humility, prayer, seeking His face, and repentance from wrongdoing.

Not the heathen, but the Lord's people are compelled to do so. It appears like much of the church is experiencing a new humility, which is encouraging. In recent years, we've seen some of the most powerful prayer movements in history. Thousands of Christians, particularly young people, are now seeking an intimate relationship with God. All of these signals are quite encouraging. However, there has been little or no repentance for the sins of the past. Even the most devoted Christian organizations have fallen to such a level of unrighteousness and the sins that the Lord labeled "wickedness" that Christians are no longer distinguishable from non-Christians in basic morality and integrity, according to in-depth investigations. The status of the church in America is awful and biblically terrifying. It happened while we were watching.

Eli had spent his entire life as a devout priest in the Lord's home. He was so devoted to the Lord that when he learned that the ark of God had been taken by the Philistines, he collapsed and died. Despite this, he received one of the Lord's harshest rebukes in the Bible. Why?

Samuel's first word from God was judgment for Eli, because he had allowed his sons to slip into wickedness and bring a curse upon themselves without rebuking them. Eli was taught in this message that no amount of sacrifices or offerings could ever atone for this wrongdoing. Even though Eli acknowledged that this was the Lord's word, he made no modifications. Eli was not told that his misdeeds could not be forgiven, but that no amount of good actions, no matter how long they were performed, could ever make up for his carelessness in failing to correct those who had been committed to his care.

This means that all of the good actions and compassion in the world will not make up for our failure to prevent those entrusted to us from falling into the iniquity and wickedness that will be their fate.

Galatians 5:19-21 Galatians Adultery, fornication, uncleanness, lasciviousness, idolatry, witchcraft, hatred, variance, emulations, wrath, strife, seditions, heresies, Envyings, murders, drunkenness, revellings, and such like: of which I have told you before, as I have also told you in the past, that they who do such things shall not inherit the kingdom of God.

If we have dedicated our life to Christ but continue to live according to the flesh as stated here, the message in the other major New Testament texts, such as the Book of Romans, is that we will perish.

The Apostle Paul forewarned believers in II Timothy 4 about a period when they would "only want to have their ears tickled" or could only hear nice things, resulting in a huge deception. Much of the church in America has now fallen into that mindset, as they instinctively reject everything they perceive to be negative. As both the Lord and His apostles forewarned, such people are doomed.

Even if their eternal lives are in risk, today's wealth of teachers and doctrines can make people feel better about themselves. Such doctrines have diluted the plain principles of Scripture to the point where they can make individuals feel at ease in their sin, but they are fooling you. Even the most faithful can make mistakes; nonetheless, they will not justify their sins, but rather repent. Repentance entails feeling remorse as well as turning away from the sin.

Doctrines are currently being propagated that the Lord no longer judges since the New Covenant was formed.

4:17 1st Peter For the time has arrived for judgment to begin at God's house; and if it begins with us, what will become of those who refuse to obey God's gospel?

The New Testament also makes it clear that those who dilute God's Word to the point of becoming stumbling stones for His people will face judgment.

As I've witnessed God's love and grace for sinners, I've been stretched far beyond my own thinking. It will be a marvel for all of eternity that He would love us so much that He would go to the cross as He did. It's amazing that we can see His patience in our own time because He doesn't want anyone to perish. Even so, as the New Testament makes plain, God's patience has a limit, and we would be naive to assume otherwise.

11:22 in Romans Consider God's goodness and severity: severity on those who fell, but goodness toward thee if thou continuest in his goodness; otherwise, thou shalt be cut off as well.

Those who only perceive His benevolence and not His severity do not see Him for who He truly is. Those who only perceive His wrath and ignore His goodness do not see Him for who He truly is. Those who see Him as He is see both kindness and severity in Him.

It has taken a long time for the Church of America to face judgment. God is a just and righteous God, and all of His judgments are just and righteous. His verdicts aren't always negative; they can also be positive, affirming what's good. They have the ability to declare both innocence and guilt. The Bible's teachings on judgment have been twisted many times, but the righteous always rejoice when He judges them.

55:12 (Isaiah) For ye shall go forth joyfully, and be led forth in peace: the mountains and hills shall sing before you, and all the trees of the field shall clap their hands.

Everyone will stand before the Judgment Seat of Christ, according to the Scriptures. This will be beneficial to the pious and detrimental to the evil.

The Bible mentions several types of God's judgment, but only condemnation and destruction are mentioned. The rest is God's discipline for those whom He loves. The most terrifying thing, according to Hebrews 12, should be if we are still living in sin and getting away with it. This implies that we are not His children. He will punish us if we are His sons.

Because He still loves America, He has been passing judgment on her, and this is proof that He has not given up on her. His judgments are becoming progressively severe, like an alarm that sounds louder and louder if we do not wake up. Some Christian leaders have more judgment than insurance firms. What these leaders have referred to as "acts of nature" are now referred to as "acts of God," and they are.

Many of the things that are being released upon the earth are the result of God's constraints being removed, allowing the world to reap what it has sown. This is evident in passages like Revelation 7. Even still, His allowing these things to happen is His judgment, and if we don't recognize it for what it is, no one will repent in time to prevent even worse things from happening.

If this offends you, you have a skewed, twisted understanding of Scripture. Such people will view what are actually acts of love as acts of condemnation. These are the untaught and unstable people Peter described as distorting the Scriptures to their own detriment. Only if we do not acknowledge and repent of the judgments will we be destroyed. God prefers to show mercy, but there are times when judgment is required, and if this does not work, destruction is the result. This is why Jesus, the Lord, weeps for Jerusalem. He would have preferred to gather her under His wings, but she rejected the time of her visitation, resulting in her destruction.

Let us repent while the judgment is still in the stage of discipline, before it becomes destructive. We are also told that we will be able to judge ourselves and that He will not be required to do so.

11:31 in 1 Corinthians We shouldn't be judged if we don't judge ourselves.

If we do not humble ourselves and fall on the Rock to be broken, the Rock will fall on us and grind us into powder, as the Lord Jesus made clear. Let's go the simple route!

The United States of America is in risk. We will not be able to survive much longer if we continue in our current path. I understand that things appear to be improving, but when men say things like "peace and safety," that is when disaster strikes. We can't gauge our progress by looking at the outside world; instead, we must examine our own hearts. If we will turn from the things that will keep us from inheriting God's kingdom, from our wicked ways, and embrace the humility that will compel us to pray and seek His face, as the rest of Galatians 5 declares:

Galatians 5:22-25 is a passage from the book of Galatians. Love, joy, peace, longsuffering, gentleness, goodness, faith, meekness, and temperance are the fruit of the Spirit, and there is no law against them. And those who belong to Christ have crucified the flesh with its passions and lusts. Let us walk in the Spirit if we live in the Spirit.

If we, God's people, choose to walk in the Spirit rather than the flesh, He will heal our land and use us to do so.

I'd like to make a point here. In our Land of the Free, we must comprehend this. The Obama administration has finalized a radical new rule that would mandate all health insurance providers to provide abortion-inducing medications, sterilization, and contraception, all at no cost, under the Affordable Care Act. The religious exemption in the rule was based on a provision crafted by the ACLU, and it applied even to religious organizations like Catholic schools, hospitals, universities, and charities that reject such activities as a matter of their belief.

NOW IS THE TIME TO RISE UP IN PRAYER AND UNITY!!!

18

~

The Early Pathways are Being Rediscovered

There are numerous open paths to which we all have complete access.

6:16 Jeremiah So says the LORD, "Stand in the ways, and see, and ask for the old paths, where the good way is, and walk in it, and your souls shall find rest." They, on the other hand, declared, "We will not walk there."

18:15 Jeremiah Because my people have forgotten me, they have burned incense to vanity, causing them to stray from the ancient routes, to walk in paths that have not been cast up;

36:2 Ezekiel Because the enemy has said against you, Aha, even the ancient high places are ours in possession, thus says the Lord GOD:

3:21 (Acts) Whom the heaven must receive until the times of restitution of all things, as God has spoken through all of his holy prophets since the beginning of time.

Jesus walked the Pathways with God and chose to follow them

even to death, paving the way for us to return to the Father in a new and living way. Through the curtain of His body, Jesus opened the Way and voluntarily offered Himself to lead us back to God. After the resurrection, he told Mary in the garden.

Revelation 20:17 Touch me not, for I have not yet ascended to my Father; but go to my brethren, and tell them, I ascend to my Father, and your Father; and to my God, and your God.

We must follow the way Jesus walked in order to return to Eden. His was a life of contemplation, prayer, devotion, and connection with the Father.

Revelation 14:5, 6 Thomas says to him, "Lord, we have no idea where you're going, and how can we know the way?" Jesus tells him, "I am the way, the truth, and the life; no one comes to the Father except through me."

The Lord God placed a cherubim with a flaming sword to keep and guard "the way" to the tree of life after Adam fell from God's glory.

22–24 in Genesis 3 And the LORD God said, Behold, the man has become like us, knowing good and evil; and now, lest he put forth his hand and take likewise of the tree of life, and eat, and live for ever: As a result, the LORD God expelled him from the Garden of Eden, commanding him to till the ground from which he was taken. So he drove the man out of the garden of Eden, and he erected Cherubims and a flaming sword that turned every which way to guard the path to the tree of life to the east.

Jesus is the final destination. He declared, "I am the Way."

1 Corinthians 15:21-24 Because man brought death, he also brought the resurrection of the dead. Because, just as everyone dies in Adam, everyone will be made alive in Christ.

Adam was created from the dust of the ground and bore the image of God. He had a wonderful friendship with the Lord, strolling and chatting with Him every day like a parent would with his son. Our connection to God was severed, but as One who bears the image of a heavenly Man, Jesus, the Heavenly Man, reopened the ancient routes. Jesus took on the nature of a Life-Giving Spirit, restoring humanity to the position from which it had fallen.

1 Corinthians 15:45-49 1 Corinthians As thus, it is written. Adam, the first man, was given a living soul, whereas Adam, the last, was given a quickening spirit. However, that which is spiritual came first, followed by that which is natural, and finally that which is spiritual. The first man is of the ground, earthy, while the second is the Lord of the heavens. As the earthy is, so are they who are earthy, and as the heavenly is, so are they who are heavenly. We will bear the image of the heavenly, just as we have carried the image of the earthy.

Enoch walked with God on the ancient paths before being taken by God.

Verse 22-24 of Genesis 5 And Enoch walked with God for three hundred years after he had Methuselah, and had sons and daughters: And Enoch lived for three hundred sixty-five years in total: And Enoch walked with God, but he was no longer with God since God had taken him.

God finally kept Enoch after he spent so much time on these supernatural highways. Enoch walked in the Heavenlies with the Lord and was aware of the vast resources available there, as well as the spirit realm's limitless dimensions. He was even requested to make atonement with the Creator on behalf of the fallen angels. As a forerunner, Enoch was given permission to see things that only a few people had seen before. Obviously, Adam was still alive during Enoch's time on earth, and I'm sure he spent a lot of time with him talking about life before the Fall. I imagine Adam telling Enoch about his stroll with the Lord in the Garden, how he moved with ease and authority. With this knowledge as a foundation, Enoch could approach God with confidence. God allowed Enoch to enter His presence with the help of the angels. He followed the ancient paths that were created just for humans. His never-ending search to know God opens doors to the sky that were previously closed to most people. Those who seek God with zeal are rewarded. Many of his revelations and contacts in the celestial realms were recorded in his journal. It was apparent that the early church had and quoted Enoch's book, and that it was highly appreciated. It was quoted by Jesus, Peter, and Jude, among others. It is similar to other known chronicles chronicling Enoch's visits to Heaven and communications with the Lord, despite the fact that it is not regarded Canon.

God has always yearned for a people who would be entirely His as family on earth, with whom He could share His heart and the secrets of the cosmos, since the beginning of time. Knowing the beginning from the end was an act worth pursuing, knowing that one day there would be a people who would not reject Him or push Him away. Following their deliverance from Egypt through miraculous signs and wonders, the children of Israel were invited as a nation to ascend the mountain and witness the glory of God as Moses did. God desired for everyone of His children to know Him and shine with His glory as Moses did, but they rejected down the Lord's invitation after three days of preparation because they were scared of His presence.

Exodus 19:1-20 is a passage from the book of Exodus. When the children of Israel were led out of Egypt in the third month, they arrived in the Sinai wilderness on the same day. They had traveled from Rephidim and arrived at the Sinai desert, where they had erected their tents in the wilderness; and Israel stayed there before the hill. And Moses went up to God, and the LORD spoke to him from the mountain, saying, Thus shalt thou say to the house of Jacob, and tell the children of Israel: You have seen what I did to the Egyptians, and how I carried you on eagles' wings, and brought you unto myself. Now, if ye will truly obey my voice and maintain my promise, ye shall be a peculiar treasure to me above other people, for the land is mine; and ye shall be a kingdom of priests and a holy nation to me. These are the words you are to speak to the children of Israel. And Moses came and summoned the elders of the people, laying before them all the words that the LORD had given him. And all of the people responded in unison, saying, "All that the LORD has declared, we will accomplish." And Moses brought the people's words to the LORD. And the LORD said to Moses, "Behold, I come to thee in a thick cloud, that the people may hear what I say to thee, and believe thee forever." And Moses reported the people's words to the LORD. And the LORD said to Moses, "Go to the people, sanctify them today and tomorrow, and let them wash their garments; and be ready for the third day, for the LORD will come down onto Mount Sinai in the face of all the people." And thou shalt set bounds around the people, saying, Take heed that ye do not go up into the mount, or touch the border of it: whosoever toucheth the mount shall surely be stoned, or shot through; whether it be beast or man, it shall not live: they shall come up to the mount when the trumpet soundeth long. And Moses descended from the mountain to the people, sanctifying them, and they washed their garments. And he told the people, "Be ready for the third day; do not come at your women." On the third day, in the morning, there were thunders and lightnings, and a thick cloud upon the mount, and the voice of the trumpet was exceedingly loud, and all the people in the camp frightened. And Moses led the people out of the tent to meet with God, and they stood at the bottom of Mount Sinai. Mount Sinai was completely engulfed in smoke because the LORD descended upon it in fire, and the smoke ascended like that of a furnace, and the entire mount trembled violently. And when the trumpet's voice became longer and louder, Moses spoke, and God spoke back to him through a voice. And the LORD descended upon Mount Sinai, upon the summit of the mountain; and the LORD summoned Moses to the summit; and Moses ascended.

The invitation was for all of Israel to come to the mountain and behold God's glory, as well as be transformed in His presence. They backed away out of dread. They were afraid of dying on the mountain if they refused God.

Exodus 20:18-21 is a passage from the book of Exodus. And when the people saw the thunderings, lightnings, trumpet boom, and the mountain smoking, they dispersed and stood distance away. They responded to Moses, "Speak to us, and we will listen; but do not speak to us about God, lest we perish." And Moses replied to the people, "Fear not; for God has come to test you, that his fear may be before your eyes, that you may not transgress." And the people stood back, and Moses approached the dense darkness where God was hiding.

Like Moses, the Lord desired for all of His people to shine with His glory. They had witnessed the might of God's miracles and wonders, as well as how God had shattered the world's most powerful nation, releasing them from slavery with supernatural authority never seen before. Even after seeing all of this, they still refused to come up into the mountain of His presence. They were simply terrified of His Majesty's might. Not far down the road, Moses had dispatched ten scouts to hunt for the country that God had promised to give the Israelites as an inheritance. The spies scouted the area for forty days. They brought fruit from the Promised Land when they returned.

Numbers 13:30-33 are a set of numbers that can be found in the Bible And Caleb brought the people to a halt in front of Moses, saying, "Let us go up immediately and possess it; because we are fully able to subdue it." But his companions remarked, "We will not be able to go up against the people; they are stronger than we." And they returned to the children of Israel with a bad report of the land that they had searched, saying, "The land through which we have gone to search it is a land that eatth up its inhabitants," and "All the people that we saw in it are men of great stature." And there we beheld the giants, the sons of Anak, who came from the giants: and we were as small as grasshoppers in our own eyes, and we were as small as grasshoppers in theirs.

Because of the giants, the people were afraid to enter the land. They discussed appointing a new commander for themselves and returning to Egypt.

Moses and Aaron, on the other hand, fell flat on their faces in front of the entire Israelite assembly. Joshua and Caleb attempted to calm the crowd and reason with them.

If the LORD is pleased with us, he will bring us into this land and give it to us, a land flowing with milk and honey. Only do not rebel against the LORD, and do not be afraid of the inhabitants of the country; for they are bread for us; their defense has been taken away from them, and the LORD is with us; do not be afraid of them.

The congregation was deafeningly deafeningly deafeningly deafeningly deafeningly deafeningly They'd made their decision. They planned to stone Joshua and Caleb with stones and devise a strategy to return to Egypt.

14:10-19 is a chapter in the book of Numbers. However, the entire congregation demanded that they be stoned. And the LORD's glory shone in the congregation's tabernacle in front of all the children of Israel. How long will this people provoke me, the LORD replied to Moses? How long will it be until they believe me, despite all the clues I've shown them? I will afflict them with plague and disinherit them, and I will make of thee a larger and more powerful people than they. Then the Egyptians will hear it,' Moses declared to the LORD (for thou broughtest up this people in thy might from among them;) And they will tell it to the people of this land, for they have heard that thou LORD is among this people, that thou LORD hath been seen face to face, that thy cloud stands over them, and that thou goest before them by day in a cloud pillar, and by night in a fire pillar. Now, if thou killst all this people as if they were one man, the countries who have heard of thy fame will speak, saying, Because the LORD was unable to deliver these people into the land that he promised them, he has slaughtered them in the wilderness. And now, I beseech thee, let the strength of my Lord be strong, as thou hast declared, saying, The LORD is longsuffering and full of mercy, forgiving iniquity and transgression and by no means clearing the guilty, visiting the fathers' sin on the children to the third and fourth generations. I implore thee, pardon this people's wrongdoing according to the grandeur of thy mercy, and in the same way that thou hast forgiven this people from Egypt until now.

The Lord was so angry with the Israelites that He told Moses that He was going to wipe them out with disease, disinherit them, and raise up a people larger and more powerful than they. Moses, on the other hand, pleaded Israel's cause to God, and God listened.

And the LORD responded, "I have pardoned according to your word," but "all the world shall be filled with the glory of the LORD as long as I live."

The Lord has had enough of them. They had witnessed His Might, Power, and Strength; they had seen His Glory. There had never been another country that God had claimed and fought for as His own. Even though they really walked through the Red Sea on dry ground, escorted by the supernatural cloud by day and the pillar of fire by night, these people refused to accept that God was capable of driving out the giants in the country and giving them respite. Moses was taught by the Lord that these people are stiff-necked. They would not believe it. If it hadn't been for Moses, God would have slaughtered them all as one man. "I have pardoned their guilt according to your promise," the Lord told Moses, "but truly as I live and as the world shall be filled with the glory of the Lord!" By His own Name, God promised that the earth would be filled with His glory. He'd have a people who wouldn't turn him down, an earthly family who knew His ways and paths, a supernatural people who knew His glory. This was the source of the Lord's wrath against Israel. He showed Himself to a stiff-necked people that refused to believe in Him time and over again. There has never been a generation in human history that has been filled with the glory of the Lord, and I believe we are that generation. We are the generation of Glory! I believe we are the ones God was waiting for to bring the knowledge of the Lord's Glory to the earth.

2:14 Habakkuk Because, as the seas cover the sea, the earth will be flooded with knowledge of the LORD's splendor.

A generation of Glory has already begun to shine with the radiance and splendor of His light. This body will not only believe in God, but will believe in God. In the world, they will appear and act like God. They will realize that they, too, are filled with the Godhead's fullness (Father, Son, and Holy Spirit), and that the Spirit of Holiness and resurrection power resides within them. As Kingdom representatives, they will become God's earthly gateway, allowing Heaven to open up to them. With this authority, they can act on God's behalf, eliminating the devil's activities and establishing Jesus' will wherever they go. As God's magistrates and judiciaries, they will be filled with revelation knowledge, knowing how to implement righteousness and justice on the earth. God was looking for a rising glory generation, and this is it. On the world, this is His Body. Yes, Jesus Christ will return in the clouds one day, at the last day trump, but He will return in and through a corporate Body of Christ in the earth before that day. Jesus paid the greatest price to bring us back into right connection with Himself, both now and in the future. He is reaping the harvest of tears sowed in Gethsemane's Garden. Because those who plant in sorrow will undoubtedly reap in joy, bringing in the sheaves. To bring us back to this realm, Jesus Christ paid a heavy price in blood. In the ear, the fruit is ripe and ready to pick. It's now or never. Jesus, who is the Tree of Life, has paved the way back to Eden.

19

~

The Fire That Doesn't Get Burned

God revealed something to me that I believe should be included in this book. Many people go through God's Fire. We need to be able to get through the flames without getting burned or hurt. I'm aware that some of what I'll say in this final section has already been discussed in other parts of the book. One of God's primary motivations for directing me to write about this topic. In Isaiah 43:2, God promises that we will not be burned, nor will the heat scorch us as we go through the fire. The following truths will help you comprehend how that promise can be kept.

The longer God keeps us in the fire and the hotter the flames, the more we'll be tempted to deny these traits of God. When God allows us to be stripped of everything and there's nothing left for us to rely on but His character, we'd best have in-depth revelation, since God can purposefully remove all other understanding in the midst of the searing ordeal. If I hadn't spent time studying God's character as a way of life, my faith could have sunk. When we're in the midst of tribulation and we're unable to recognize His voice, we have nothing left to cling to or hang our trust on. The confusion test is the most difficult of all. Perplexing and depressing conditions have occurred frequently and consistently in every other trial.

4:8 in 2 Corinthians We are afflicted on all sides, but not distressed; confused, but not hopeless; Romans 11:33 The treasures of God's wisdom and knowledge are immeasurable! How impenetrable his judgments are, and how impenetrable his paths are!

But my faith hasn't been shaken because the revelation of God's character is more powerful than everything thrown at me to persuade me otherwise. Moreover, God has dependably sent me the exact word I needed to hear on several occasions during the continuous agony, weakness, sleeplessness, and perplexities. God's sensitivity and infinite comprehension have been demonstrated in the timing of these love offerings.

145:17 in Psalms In all of his ways, the LORD is righteous, and all of his handiwork are holy.

Isaiah 50:10, 11 is a prophecy from the prophet Isaiah. Who among you is afraid of the LORD, who obeys his servant's words, who walks in the dark and has no light? Let him put his hope in the LORD's name and cling to his God. Walk in the light of your fire and the sparks that ye have lit, all ye who kindle a fire and compass themselves about with sparks. You shall have this from my hand, and you shall weep.

No matter how dark and puzzling the circumstances, it always pays to maintain trusting God's unwavering faithfulness, infinite wisdom and knowledge, absolute justice, and unfathomable love. He hasn't given up His throne, is in complete control, and is aware of your location.

16:8, 9 (Psalms) I have set the LORD always before me; I will not be moved because he is at my right hand. As a result, my heart rejoices, and my glory rejoices; my flesh, too, will rest in hope.

34:1 (Psalms) David's psalm when he changed his behavior in front of Abimelech, who drove him away and sent him away. I will always bless the LORD, and my mouth will be filled with his praise.

It will not only help us maintain our focus and perspective, but it may also help us maintain our sanity, as it did mine. It's also a potent weapon in spiritual combat.

20:22 in 2 Chronicles The LORD arranged ambushments against the children of Ammon, Moab, and Mount Seir, who had come against Judah, and they were struck.

149:5, 6 Psalms Let the Christians rejoice in their splendour and sing joyfully in their beds. Let their mouths be filled with God's praises, and their hands be armed with a two-edged sword;

Paul writes to the Ephesians in Ephesians 6:10-18. Finally, dear brothers and sisters, be strong in the Lord and in his might. Put on the complete armor of God so that you can stand against the devil's schemes. We are fighting against principalities, powers, rulers of the darkness of this world, and spiritual wickedness in high places, not against flesh and blood. Take up therefore the full armour of God, that ye may be able to resist in the evil day, and having done everything, to stand. As a result, stand with your loins girt with truth and your breastplate of righteousness on; And your feet shod with the gospel of peace preparation; above all, taking the shield of faith, with which ye shall be able to quench all the wicked's fiery darts. Take the salvation helmet and the sword of the Spirit, which is God's word: David took the initiative in his battle with Goliath by announcing his confidence in the name of the Lord of hosts. He prayed with all prayer and supplication in the Spirit, and he watched over it with all perseverance and supplication for all the saints. Then David dashed to confront the Philistine colossus. Either the devil is bothering us or we are bothering him. Before he can attack us, be on the offensive every day and resist him in Jesus' name.

Be alert, for your opponent, the devil, walks around like a roaring lion, seeking whom he may devour: Who resist steadfastly in the faith, knowing that your brethren in the world are suffering the same trials.

If we believe we can, God may make it hotter until we realize we can't. So make the decision right now to be vulnerable enough to admit your vulnerability and ask for help. In the garden of Gethsemane, Jesus did it three times. When He was experiencing the agony of being separated from His Father during His moment of greatest need, He begged for prayer support from some of His closest companions. This involved becoming sin for all sinners and suffering the agony of crucifixion.

1:19 Philippians Because I know that via your prayers and the supply of the Holy Spirit, this will lead to my salvation.

4:3, 4 Colossians Also praying for us, that God would open a channel of expression for us, that we may communicate the mystery of Christ, for which I am also bound: that I might make it visible as I ought to say.

David claimed that he would have died in his agony if it hadn't been for his delight in God's Word.

You'll watch Him regulate the temperature according to His divine purpose, not because He's irrational or arbitrary. He's indicating to you that He's aware of your situation. He's in command. I've seen this fact many times, and whenever the anguish has been lifted sovereignly and briefly, I've always seen God's reasons in doing so. It's been simply extraordinary.

20

꩜

Making the Decision to Follow God's Plan

Many people declare they want to be a part of God's plan until they learn how much it will cost them. Regardless of the cost, we must choose to be a part of His plan.

Balaam had a choice when Balak took him up to the mountain and allowed him to gaze down and see the Israelites in the wilderness. Balaam had the option of either cursing the Israelites or coming down from his high and lofty perch to assist them.

It's entirely up to you. Will the Church choose to help the people from its high and lofty arrogant places, or will it continue to try to curse them? It's entirely up to you. You're the Church, after all. So, what are you going to do? What do you want to be recognized for in your life? It's past time for us to acknowledge that the spirit of Balaam has infiltrated the modern Church. It's past time we recognized it and drove it out, but ultimately, the decision is yours.

People begin to hunt for reasons to leave churches. If people are truly mature, they will persevere in doing what God wants them to do, rather than what is easiest. The point was that if you didn't want to be a Christian who wanted to grow in the Lord, he would give you an excuse to go because he wanted people in his church who wanted to move forward with the Lord.

We, as a Church, must quit being immature Christians and take the next step toward maturity. All of this backbiting and gossip makes me feel like I'm in a kindergarten classroom. "She hit me!" can you hear the echoes of children's laughter and tears? In the Kingdom, we need to stop acting like 5-year-olds and start acting like adult sons and daughters.

8:14 in Romans They are sons of God to the extent that they are directed by the Spirit of God.

8:19 (Romans) Because the creature's genuine expectation is for the manifestation of God's sons.

The whole of creation is eagerly anticipating the appearance of God's sons. That means we must take responsibility for our sonship. In the Kingdom, we must choose to mature and stop acting like immature children.

It is a choice to grow spiritually. It makes no difference how long you've been saved or how many people you've led to Christ. It's about making the decision to grow up with God and move on. As time passes and God places experiences in front of you, you choose to mature. We must make the decision to be the mature sons and daughters that God has destined us to be. We must make the decision to mature and stop moaning and griping about who said what. Is it really that important in the larger scheme of things that that individual injured you? Don't be concerned about what they've done or are doing. You should be worried about yourself.

2 Corinthians 2:12 Therefore, my beloved, work out your own salvation with fear and trembling, as you have always obeyed, not only in my presence, but now much more in my absence.

You must figure out how to save yourself. You won't be working out your brother's or sister's, but you will be working out your own. So, instead of focusing on others, focus on yourself!

I've got some good news for you. If you spend any amount of time in a church, you will find dozens of things to be angry about. You'll discover a plethora of things to critique. Trying to hold on to all of those things will only prevent you from finishing your race.

"These are days of transformation," I've heard over and over on the prophetic wave. Change occurs when we begin to move in unison! This isn't only something I've heard for my personal life; it's been reaffirmed by prophetic voice after prophetic voice throughout the Body of Christ. But hold on a second! Things from our past are dragging us down, therefore we're wearing ankle weights. What are we expected to do if we can't swim? It's time to ditch the ankle weights and go swimming.

Why do humans cling to "weights" or relics from the past, such as sacred artifacts? I believe it is sometimes because we deceive ourselves into believing that by clinging to the past, we are retaining some level of control. Fear is at the root of it all. If we let go, we will have to completely trust God, which might be a scary prospect. If you have a true revelation of who God is, you should be able to trust Him by now.

Not that I have already attained all of this or been perfected, but I press on to grasp what Christ Jesus has taken hold of me for.

3:13–14 in Philippians I do not consider myself to have comprehended, brethren: but this one thing I do: forgetting what is behind and reaching forward to what is ahead, I press forward the mark for the prize of the high calling of God in Christ Jesus.

You must let go in order to move on. You must put the past behind you. Most of the time, we think to ourselves, "How am I expected to do that?" when we hear the word forget. I can't seem to recall what happened. That event or moment will never be forgotten in my mind. It has the potential to set off a massive cycle of self-loathing.

While you can't forget the incident, you can forget the feelings that surrounding it like a tidal wave, as I've frequently stated. Worry and anxiety are signs that you aren't trusting God.

4:6 Philippians Don't be concerned about anything; instead, make your requests known to God through prayer and petition with thankfulness.

We must remove the ankle weights in order to completely begin to swim in this change and unification that God is taking us into. We must have faith in what God is doing. We must make the decision to let go of the past and embrace the future. I understand how frightening that might be.

I used to work out with ankle weights, and after a while you forget they're even there. You've become so accustomed to being burdened that you have forgotten what it's like to be free of them.

In the name of Jesus, be set free from them. Allow God to take away your worries and cares. Allow God to take away the burdens of both pleasant and negative memories. Memories aren't necessarily awful, but you can't cling to them like a life raft and expect to swim to the places you need to go. You must now let go and trust in God's protection. He will never abandon you or abandon you. His views about you are positive, and He has great plans for you in this season. I know it will be worth it if you choose to let the weights go. God is delighted about your prospects. Join in the fun with Him.

When someone injure and offend you, you can't flee and hide. This only serves to inflame the situation. When you need to confront it, do so, but keep choosing to let it go. You're being held back by your ankle weights!

Choose not to unload and gossip when you want to. There are times when you need to speak up, but for the most part, keep your mouth shut. Stop trying to manipulate people's emotions and feelings; it's not worth it. If you're not careful, running your mouth will eventually bite you in the behind.

You must become a blessing to people who are close to you. Unless you're willing to be a blessing to others, stop looking for a blessing for yourself. I'll admit that I'm a touch introverted at times. I'll admit that there are times when I don't want to be overly social. I have to force myself to be more outgoing at times. But each time I do, I'm glad I did. Seed season and harvest have a spiritual significance. It's as though you're a farmer yourself. Seeds are planted in the ground, and those seeds are watered. You reap what you sow when the seed sprouts into a tree that breaks out of the earth and bears fruit. "What goes around comes around," as the saying goes.

This is something you can observe in your own life. What seeds have you planted in the Church's relationships? Have you sowing a lot of apathy? Are you beginning to wonder why you feel as if no one cares about you? Please excuse me, but I believe it's because your disinterest is visible. Have you sown a forest of rumor about you?

The seeds you've sowed in the past have brought you to where you are now. Start sowing good seeds today if you want positive things to happen to you. Start saying nice things about the people in your life. When you want to bash someone, start complimenting them. Don't say anything if you don't have anything nice to say.

The best thing that could be said about them, according to one eulogy, was that they had good teeth. Wow! That sums up all of life's achievements. Teeth in good condition.

There are moments in the Church when we must correct, and I would be remiss if I didn't bring this up in this message. The Bible explicitly tells us not to associate with those who promote strife and division in our communities and churches.

I implore you, brethren, to be wary of individuals who sow dissensions, difficulties, and divides in your midst, in direct contrast to the doctrine (teaching) that you have been taught. Many people are wondering, "What about love?" God still loves the individual, but you become a product of the company with which you associate. You can love these people, pray for them, and be a benefit to them, but the Bible makes it clear that you must be cautious around them. That doesn't mean you should treat them badly. However, it necessitates vigilance. Allowing someone into your inner circle isn't always a good idea. When you are constantly exposed to negativity, it will eventually influence you. There is no such thing as an island. People need to be in the company of others who encourage them. It's time to make new friends if you don't want to be like your current buddies. I'm not saying you can't love your old pals, but you should always seek out companions who inspire you to grow closer to God. You always want a group of pals that will give you the truth about love and not sugarcoat it.

Tough love is sometimes necessary in churches. It's not that people don't love the individual, but we can't allow habitual immorality fester in the life of a church member and do nothing about it. If a complaint against a leader isn't backed up by two or three credible witnesses, disregard it. If someone commits a sin, call them to the carpet. Those that are inclined in that direction will immediately recognize that they will not be able to get away with it.

1 Timothy 5:19-22 Rather than an allegation, an elder is brought before two or three witnesses. Rebuke those who sin in front of everyone so that others may be afraid.

The congregation can see what's going on and is terrified of falling into this pattern of wrongdoing. It's also so that those who have a tendency of sinning would see the folly of their ways and finally return to the Church. Remember, God must discipline His beloved children, just as I would reprimand my child if he ran into an electrical outlet while wearing steel wool. Discipline is an expression of love. Discipline in the Church can sometimes entail removing persons from positions of leadership for a period of time. If they're truly dealing with severe issues, they should devote their efforts to improving their own lives rather than sowing into the lives of others. Other toddlers are watching him, as well as you, to see how you respond. If you don't deal with a problem with steel wool or sin right away, you can end up with a swarm of others who think it's OK to do the same thing. Unless specific activities are taken, the fear and reverence for the Lord will be diluted.

If we're going to quit cursing our Christian brothers and sisters, we need to start treating others the way we want to be treated. That is something Jesus taught us to do, but it appears that this principle has been lost in the Church through the decades. We're so preoccupied with obtaining some supernatural revelation or God encounter that we've relegated the Golden Rule's core concept to a dusty, filthy shelf, barely noticing it. Remove it from the shelf! We're all fascinated by signs and wonders. We all enjoy the supernatural, but in order for the commanded blessing to come to us, we must be in agreement.

We want to see signs, wonders, and miracles, but our compassion has grown stale and lukewarm. It's time to begin praying that God will awaken us from our slumber. I believe that the Church in America is entering a period in which we will have to start relying on one another and coming together in ways that we have never seen before in contemporary Church history. People in this country have reached a standstill, believing that we don't need to support one another since our government will. In this country, we've adopted a welfare mentality that says we don't need to do anything because the government will take care of everything.

I'm sorry to inform you, Church, that our government has reached new heights of over-extension. Our government is not the world's rescuer. Our Savior is Jesus Christ. We, the Church, have the responsibility of being Jesus' hands and feet on the ground. I feel that the churches will become increasingly important to the people of our country. I believe we are entering a season in the modern Church when people will flock to the Kingdom in large numbers, similar to the Acts church.

Be prepared for 50 people if you're used to ten people giving their lives to the Lord in one service. Prepare for 500 people if you're used to 50 people in a single service. Churches that have sold themselves out to God in this world will see a multiplication. A flood of souls is entering the Kingdom, and the churches that God has formed must prepare for all of these new believers. Will we be able to cope? Will we be able to love them without condition? Will we be able to assist them in their spiritual development? Will we be so preoccupied with our own goals that we walk right past them, ignoring their cries for help?

It's absurd to consider abandoning a physical infant to her fate. It would and should be a felony if I left a baby alone in a house for a few days. That is something for which people should be arrested. However, we believe it is OK to leave all of these spiritual newborns in the Church to fend for themselves. No! These new and young Christians require our assistance. They need us to come down from our lofty perches and assist them in their spiritual development. In these days, the world is crying out for spiritual moms and fathers to step forth. We need people who will put aside their egos and be prepared to invest in others so that they might achieve more success than we achieved.

Jesus was a firm believer in investing His life in others. Jesus instilled His life in a large number of people, primarily His 12 disciples. The world was revolutionized by those 12 disciples. They were game-changers on a global scale. Those 12 disciples went on to pour themselves into a large number of others, raising a large number of sons and daughters in the process. Jesus had only one life, but He multiplied Himself many times over. That is something we must do with others around us.

Years ago, I recall arguing with God, telling Him that I was only one person, and that I couldn't possibly make a difference. I believe that most persons called to ministry have had that talk with God at some point. It was as though God's words were thrown at me like a hefty trench coat. "But God, I'm only one person," I could hear myself exclaim.

One person can make a significant difference. Jesus was a single individual. He had a significant impact. Stop telling God that the problem is too large for him to handle. Stop staring at your issue. The more you think about it, the greater it becomes. God is far bigger than the issue. Keep your gaze fixed on God. Allow God to grow larger than your anxieties! You are a single person, but you have the life of God within you. You have the ability to and will make a difference.

21

~

The Vision of the Anointed Eagles

During a Waves of Revival meeting in Belleville, Illinois, a vision was released.

Lord, thank you.

I'd never seen anything like it before, yet in the vision's river, this scripture was floating on top in letters. And how I bore you on eagle's wings and brought you unto myself, declares Exodus 19:4. And believe me when I tell you that this is one of those profound details that only occurs when I'm in a trance-like condition. I can see people all around me in the vision. I'm aware of what's going on. However, while I'm looking, I'm watching a movie. I may be staring at you and seeing this event unfolding in my head, and you're just a hazy image that I can still see. And believe me when I say it happens out of nowhere. It's not like I'm begging to be let in. It's as though I began pressing into God and was immediately drawn in, halleluiah. I was given this title and was whisked away into a trance-like state in a matter of moments. Right now, we're entering a season of delving deep into the domain of the spirit, and I mean very deep into the realm of the spirit. My body was still, but my spirit was on the go. It seemed as though I were following the Lord from place to place. I was on my way to finding something amazing. The first thing I saw was a crystal clear river, similar to those found in Destin, Florida, where the ocean is so blue that you can see the bottom in most spots. It's stunning, crystal clear, not blue, but clear, and the water was crystal clear as well. It was gushing from a massive throne, which appeared to have multiple levels. And I'm not sure what this implies other than the throne, which I suppose was the Lord's throne but which had numerous levels at the same time. It seemed like a mountain, or a successive level of His throne. And it appeared as if we could scale it. But we couldn't, and I can still see it now that I'm talking about it. The river was deep and quickly flowing, and I knew there was salvation somewhere in these waters. There was an air of liberation. And the river is brimming with provisions. And each level had to be completed in its entirety. We'll be climbing later, and it'll lead us to another level, and then another level, and so on. Before moving on to the next level, we must first claim the provision from the previous level. The spinning of the water releases a tangible anointing and glory, which I imagined was released by the Spirit as the water swirled. In this trance, I was reminded that it was similar to the angels stirring the pools of Bethesda. I noticed a bald eagle in the sky. The eagle was completely white. Everything about a white eagle was white, from the head to the feet. It was, however, an eagle. It was flying by, and I felt it had a message for me. A prophet or prophetic seeing anointing is like an eagle. God talks to me in this manner every time. And God said, "This is the day I'm going to give my eagles my message." And I believe the bird was sending the Bride a message of enlightenment. And as I watched, a white dove came in over the churning waters to join the eagle, and the dove followed the eagle faster and faster.

Representation. Of course, the dove represents the Holy Spirit. God talked to the eagles during the soaking service. And it was only a small piece of the whole that stated we would rise up on eagle's wings. And now, after all this time, God is finally revealing it because we have crossed over to the next level. And then a voice said, "First comes the Prophet." Then there was the dove. This prophetic message is familiar to me because it was spoken to me in previous visions. The Prophet is the first to appear. The dove then appears. The term prophet will be useful. What does that mean, you might ask? This was shown to me in a vision many years ago, and William Branham, a minister who preached and with evidence, had an angel who would stand alongside him and pour words of knowledge into his ear, which he would then unleash, and people were healed by the masses. In our country, he was renowned as the prophet. If he stated something, all of our country's churches adjusted correspondingly. And this is the vision I'm talking about with William Branham from before. I had a vision in which I saw him standing there with what appeared to be a halo, but he stated it was an angel standing alongside him. And it's as if he was frozen in that photo, and as he unfroze, he looked to me and said, "Bill, I want people to take my mantel." My mantel is still standing, even though I'm no longer alive. As a result, every time it said here prophet with assistance, I was remembered. Angels, you see, may communicate with us. See, we only think we can see and understand here, but it's not just hearing that we need, but also help and heavenly hosts. The voice went on to say that the dove signified a true, authentic Holy Spirit baptism. How many people are aware that today's Baptism of the Holy Spirit is not what God intended it to be? We should be walking in miracles now that we have the Holy Spirit. The Bride wade out into the deeper insight, as I call the next step of this. By the way, we're the Bride. The deep waters enticing the Bride, I realized, signified the profound insights and mysteries that the Bride of Christ has been asked to wade through. As the waves wash over her, God's message is revealed, and it is being revealed right now to her in increasingly intimate ways. I was glancing up again when I noticed the eagle circling a huge blue ball. I could see the continents' contours. I saw the continents of the earth through the Spirit. As the eagle swarmed over the globe, I saw continents light up. The white dove followed closely behind the eagle as it proceeded to circle the globe. Another white bird emerged out of nowhere, but it was considerably larger than the first. Then there was the dove. It had the bodily structure of an eagle, but his feathers were pure white, as if it came from another world. I'm talking about pure white. Although the first eagle was white, it was not completely white. When compared to the brightest white-white you could imagine, it was like an off-white. This eagle has a halo around it. It's a white eagle!!!, another white eagle!, I said without saying. The Lord's angel appears. An angel clad in white entered the scene. I could tell he wasn't just any angel, and that he wielded a lot of power. I was occasionally able to converse with the angels in the room without saying anything. It's a bizarre thing, but I can do it on occasion. I was asked if I was familiar with an angel's white eagle. The angel said that seeing him was more essential than understanding what he was there for right now. The angel then began to instruct me on how to be patient. I realized that God was dealing with me in the manner of a tiny child, painstakingly repeating information as if I didn't understand, even though I knew. He was carefully saying, "This is what this is for," but he wasn't describing the gigantic eagle. He was behaving as if I were a small child. They reminded me that the first eagle arrived with the dove, a sort of prophet guiding the way, a true Holy Spirit infilling. Paul's letter to the Ephesians (Ephesians 1:13-14) After hearing the word of truth, the gospel of your salvation, and believing that you were sealed with the Holy Spirit, you were given a promise that is the earnest of our inheritance till the redemption, the purchased property unto the praise of His glory. In terms of the actual infilling of the Holy Spirit, I feel this is what the Lord was attempting to convey in this vision. We haven't yet encountered another level of Pentecostal blessing and sensation. There's more to it than merely fill. The baptism that is about to come upon us will result in a genuine change in a believer's life, not just another man-made denomination or religious system. This moment, not included in this vision, will be very different from any other time in the realm of My Spirit infilling. So, by this time, I'm wading in the water, and I'm thinking to myself, "I mean, we're going to be filled with the Holy Spirit?" He was correct. And we're set to get filled all over again in the next weeks. And it'll be something new and exciting. The disciples had already experienced miracles, had laid hands on people, and witnessed marvels. They also requested that they be able to heal by reaching out their hand. They called for boldness, and instead received a fresh infusion of the Holy Spirit. They had already been taken. There's still more filling to be done. Remember that the dove was trailing the first eagle. The dove is now leading the eagle. The Lord's angel indicated that real Holy Spirit baptism would pave the way for the white eagle, the dazzling one that I had never understood. He also claimed that the white eagle indicated a revelation of Jesus Christ's fullness. Not simply a deeper understanding of Him, but an indwelling of Jesus Christ's actual character and virtue. To put it another way, it was meant to pass the other eagle. As a result, we resembled the white eagle, but not quite. They claimed that He wishes for us to unite. We'll be able to make it. This revelation will result in the resurrection of a live word. Many men and women of God, not just one man, Jesus Christ, are rising up as anointed eagles. This message would serve as a plumb line measuring device to determine the accuracy of all the words sent to Jesus Christ's end-time Bride. This is what we are being prepared to be, the eagle-like end-time bride. I spoke up in front of all who could hear me, saying that the world had never seen anything like the Bride. And this is what God had to say: It will be mocked and rejected by fools. It will be scorned by certain religious leaders, but it will be welcomed with joy by His genuine Bride. Then there's the next thing, a fresh thing, (Isn't that what God has been saying all along?) God has said that it is time for the Bride's revival, that it is time for the Bride's revival. These remarks, I believe, were referring to the Lord doing something new, something that will not follow historical revival patterns but rather have its own model and administration. It will be a development of Jesus Christ's ministry paradigm as depicted in the gospels. It will be authority and power operating and obeying in a corporate body of believers chosen for this purpose long before the earth was created. Then I overheard Him utter something strange to me. On Mt. Zion, things have become stuck. The Saints are in a bind. They've climbed as far as they can and don't appear to be able to progress any further into Jesus' virtues and attitudes. He went on to say that I shouldn't be concerned because it's not up to me to be concerned about them, but rather about Him. Mt. Zion, according to God, is on the other side of the throne. I asked what that meant, and he explained that Mt. Zion is the destination for everyone in the body of Christ. That was yesterday's glory, according to God. That is in the past tense. That, God says, is only the beginning of where I want My body to go. As a result, it's hidden behind the throne. New levels that are above Mt. Zion are in front of His throne. Suddenly, a majestic pyramid shape appeared in front of me, and God exclaimed, "This is Mt. Zion." But, God, the last time I saw a pyramid in the Spirit, it signified religion, I said. Yes, God says. To the body of Christ, Mt. Zion has become a pyramid. They can only go so far before giving up. I noticed a mountain as I got closer. The eagle is still flying around the blue ball of the continents, and the Holy Spirit is still leading it. And the other eagles are merging into one, as is the throne with numerous tiers, but I shift my gaze to the side. It's as if you could reach the throne levels, but God said it wasn't the path we needed to take. We must ascend the mountain. He mentioned there was a mountain where it appeared you had to climb just a few small cliffs here and there, which we did. And as I got closer, I noticed some saints. It included some of you. Some had progressed further up the mountain than others, but all were making steady progress toward the summit. I was getting a closer look than I'd ever had before, and I could see the rocky, jagged terrain and the roughness of the hills. When individuals grabbed little rocks, they would tumble off. To put it another way, those rocks may lead you to tumble. So, if you try to go too fast every time, you can tumble. Before you started reaching for a higher position, you had to be sure you were safe. There are numerous details. There are also enormous unstable rocks that would come from those above, and those boulders would just roll over the top, forcing you to hide in a gap in the rock. Powerful. You'd get hit if you didn't. Some climbers might be knocked to the bottom by these rocks and stones. Some would simply get back up and begin climbing again. Some had progressed to the point where they were unable to traverse obstacles, while others had to come to a halt since there was no longer any place to gain a footing or even dig in with their hands and lift themselves higher. And I saw the difficulty that had begun to come with those who were climbing this mountain by the Spirit as I was viewing it. They were getting increasingly stuck, with no apparent route around the stumbling block, and the most of them would be forced to retreat and re-navigate. My anguish for these folks was jolted by the angel of the Lord's words, "Don't worry." Remember what God instructed us recently in ministry: "Don't wait for anyone." Simply leave. I've spent my entire ministry waiting for everyone to get it before moving on to the next level, but God has told me not to wait any longer in the last several months. Go. Leave them, he urged. If they are unable to go to the next level, they should leave. Allow me to take care of them. The dove gives you new energy to climb. They will be stranded for a long time due to the most difficult climbing. And with the correct tools, it seemed as if I could see tools appearing on the mountain, swirling like a dove, to chisel out your next climbing position. It took time to dig yourself out of your pit, your mess, and your battle, but with the right tools, you were able to do it. And if you had to go down at all, it was only to find a different way out. Details. It was the little white dove circling the top of the mountain that I noticed a flash of movement overhead. A new anointing began to fall, and I knew it was being released by the dove's presence. Suddenly, I noticed a clear word imbedded in the stone of the mountain's face, and it read: Eagle. It looked as if someone had carved the word Eagle onto the icicles. That's how "The Anointed Eagles" came to be. The Christians began to yell and delight at the new anointing, which I overheard. Those who had been vanquished and were unable to move began to shout and say, "We can do it now!" Please, don't make me laugh. We've got this. Please, don't make me laugh. And I delighted with a new anointing, which fell upon them like a blanket, and they began shouting to those below, "We can make it!" Continue ascending. There was a response. How did you figure that out? Back up, as if they were attempting to warn them that things were about to get worse. The dove was still circling the mountain, as everyone could see. Someone else was approaching in the distance. Someone shouted from the top of the mountain as it got closer. The white eagle is displaying the single eagle. And I was worried about the saints at the bottom of the mountain, who I thought would be unable to make it to the top due to the late hour, so I wondered aloud, "How will they ever make it?" Those who refused to give up. There were still bodies at the bottom of the well who had given up. Those who merely kept saying, on the other hand, may have been exhausted. They could have been frail. They could have been annoyed. But that eagle swooped down and began picking them up one by one, escorting them to the next level. He nudged the saints as he jumped down the side of the mountain near the top, pushing them to climb, and then he would land them in another location and kind of just hit them, like, come on. And God began to reveal to me that this eagle was no longer just a white, white bird, but the eagle that had become one. I could hear the eagle (I never heard an eagle talk but in this one the eagle got to talk.) When you've climbed as high as you can, I'll carry you to the peak of Zion on my wings. And I enquired of the Lord. You said Mt. Zion was simply old junk, I said to God. Yes, this is a new Zion, a new location, a new level, he said. The Bride will be victorious. I'll share my virtues with her. The rest of the journey will be carried by me. I will carry you to the top of the mountain, just as I bore Israel out of Egypt on my wings. I screamed with the rest of the Saints, "Eagle, just take us on your wings!" And I knew in my heart that this would not be a quick fix. The wings hoist you up and carry you over that hunk, but not all the way to the top. They may carry you to the top and show you what's going on there, but then He returns you to the next level. None of the lessons, preparations, or impartations would be allowed to be skipped. Only at the hour when we couldn't climb any higher on our own would we bear up. It would have also signaled the end of all human striving to achieve the status of overcomers. And there would be a new area where we would be completely reliant on the Lord Jesus Christ. The truth is, these aren't by-passes provided by God. Even those who have given up are carried. God is the one who has pushed. Don't be concerned, he said. If they are left behind but remain with Him in their hearts, He will continue to pushing and pulling them higher. Come on, you say. You've got this. You've got this. I pray that now, as we enter a season of revelation, we will be lifted to the summit of this new mountain and seated with our beloved Bridegroom on His throne. He wants to move us to a new dimension. I wish to anoint the eagles, God declares. The eagles are our name. Lord, thank you! Halleluiah! It's all for God's glory!

22

⌒

The Vision of the Warrior Eagle

I witnessed an eagle with a wing spread that was far longer than its regular wing span. From left to right, the wing span seemed to stretch for kilometers. When the wings spread out, they appeared to stretch for miles. The Eagle's body was incredibly strong, and the Eagle's head was that of a Dove. And there was a crown on top of the Dove's head, a very lovely crown that was actually part of the Eagle. It had a horn in its mouth. A gavel, similar to what a judge would use, was in the claw of the Eagle's right hand. And I saw a swarm of eagles descend and fly above a wheat field. Oil poured out of its wings. Each piece and portion was quite powerful, but as I dug further, it seemed as though God would give me one piece at a time, and I would only see that for a short period. Then he'd add another piece, and I saw the Eagle with a massive blade strapped to its body. In the natural, I came to believe that this was simply God revealing Himself to me. But then I noticed that this Eagle was not alone in the sky. And then I looked up, and there was a flock of these Eagles, shaped like a diamond, flying through the sky, just as the birds fly south for the winter. They had the same crown, the same head, the same gavels, and the same swords, and they produced hundreds if not thousands upon thousands, shaped like a diamond. I also heard the Lord say to me, "I am rising up the Eagle warriors." They'll have the same appearance as I do. They'll flow like I do. You are progressing swiftly, according to God. God says, "I want you to be the heir to My throne." My supreme royalty is something I want you to carry. I want you to be guided by My Spirit, with your head in the lead at all times. Allow your mouth to blow the trumpet, sounding the sirens when necessary. I want you to be able to extend your wings over the harvest and discharge My anointing oil. I want you to be able to draw your sword at any time and sever the giants that stand in the way of the land. I want you to be the one who strikes the earth with the gavel of judgment. That's when you'll have to make a decision, and it'll be up to Me to bring the hammer down and say, "You've come this far, but you're not going any farther." I'm rising up ones who will say YES!, says the Lord. Don't assume this is a little matter. This is a huge part of what God is saying, that we will walk in a level of authority and mantels that are beyond our comprehension. And I noticed this Eagle flying over some places of the globe. And the swarming Eagles synchronized their movements. The Eagle's mass was always in the shape of a diamond. There was no one who disagreed that whenever you see birds migrating south for the winter, there usually appears to be a scatter somewhere, or birds eating French fries in a parking lot or whatever. You can tell they've come to a halt because they're out of sync. But in this sight, everything was in perfect sync, and they were all moving in the same direction because the Holy Spirit's head was in front of each Eagle, leading them. So when one of them turned left, they all turned left, and when one of them came to a halt and hovered over a place, they all came to a halt and lingered over that location.

When it states in My Word that they did signs and wonders, the Lord spoke to my heart and said, "I want you to consider this." Miracles, signs, and wonders abounded. According to the Lord, you will be ones in whom My very presence, which I have in you, will hover over and around My people. It looked as if everyone had gathered to watch the Eagles take flight. People would congregate and wait for the Eagles to pass by and fly over them. And I saw by the Spirit of God, and the vision is expanding even as I speak. Thank you, Lord. I saw landing ships out in the middle of the ocean, similar to how the Air Force has landing ships out in the middle of the ocean. God says it would be regarded chambers out in the waves because I saw Eagles coming down and settling on these ships. In the days ahead, God says I'm going to perform a movement out on the waters. On land, no. It will take place on the water. It will be for my people who are called by my name and who have been assigned to this hour. They'll go there to sharpen their swords. To re-energize their spirits. To acquire the relaxation and rejuvenation that is required. And the Lord says that these are the ones who will experience a revival on the water, and that when they take flight again, they will be stronger and more equipped than they have ever been. And the Lord explains that this will not be a single landing ship, but a fleet of landing ships, since it will need to be able to hold a large number of the generals that God is raising up at this time. Because it's Jesus being replicated of Himself, the Lord says every Eagle will be as if Smith Wigglesworth, Kathryn Kuhlman, and all the world's great wonders are all rolled into one. They're supposed to soar through the sky like eagles. We're expected to be able to walk in this kind of authority, and the Lord says you're already receiving a stronger anointing, and I'm going to start placing my crowns on you. I'm going to start putting trumpets in your mouth so you can sound the alarm when it's time. Halleluiah. And the Lord says I'm going to put the gavels in your hands, and anytime someone does something wrong by the Spirit's way, you're going to set it down and say NO MORE, and the Lord says this will be a strength that comes in numbers because you'll know who is just like you. You'll be able to see it when you're in the Spirit. Because there will be many people who are just like you who you will not even realize have been a part of it. They may not have been physically present with you, but they were present in spirit, according to the Lord. Now, as these Eagles were flying, I suddenly saw one main Eagle flying in the midst of everything, and I know that is Jesus Himself, as I saw it via the Spirit. But then it was as if I watched shadows of Him radiate forth, causing the masses of Eagles to be replicated of Himself. Then I noticed assignments being placed on Eagles, and when they took flight again, I noticed they reproduced themselves. God states that once you find yourself in Me, I don't only want to reproduce Myself; I want to reproduce you. When you're in Me and I'm in you, it's a beautiful thing. Then I want you to be able to separate, and the Lord says these are the ones with full mantels. These are the ones who have complete control. These are the ones who can connect with My Spirit at any time and perform any miracle that is required at the time. And the Lord promises it will continue to become larger and larger. And there will come a time when the Eagles will assemble. They will assemble in My name. They will congregate in locations where I have never gone before, for I have promised to cover the earth with My Glory. This isn't about titles, I don't believe. I don't believe this is a matter of rank. This is about just becoming a part of God's overall mission for us. Sharpen! This hour is for you to sharpen your skills. Make your sword as sharp as possible. Prepare for a time when you will be in flight for years at a time because you will go and go and go until I tell you it's time to land and rest. The Lord declares that there are many eagles. God adds, "My purpose is to have a hundred thousand Eagles with this type of anointing and strength." It's possible that they're not all bound by the same denominational agreement. It's possible that they're not in the same ministry. They may or may not be listed under this or that title. They will, however, be Eagles because the Lord has said, "I am handpicking from of the remnant of people." The Lord says that I shall look down on the body of Christ, which may number in the hundreds, and reach down and remove one person out of the entire mass. Who is it that says yes? You must understand, my children, that when you become this type of Eagle, you may fall from a greater vantage point. It's more important than ever before that you don't fall out of the sky since you're flying from a higher altitude. Someone can walk out the door and trip and fall, skinning their knee, according to God. They have the ability to run off the roof and break a leg. They can jump out of a certain plane and cut many bones in their bodies if they land just so. They can, however, climb to the highest plain above the clouds in the unseen, which is a high point where falling means death. You say, "Oh, that's too much to bear." You were the one I chose. You didn't pick Me. Many militants enlisted in the military despite having no desire to be a Green Beret. Their desires were not to be the people who had been assigned to them. They possessed a rare gift, a special capacity, or even a potential, if you will, to be picked for this honor. God says, "I'm putting authority and status stripes on your shoulders." This is why so many of you were turned down. You've been rejected by a lot of people, a lot of transfers, a lot of advancements, a lot of stuff. But the Lord adds, "I chose you for this hour precisely." Then I noticed these Eagles flying together in the Spirit. They were multi-colored, and while no two of them appeared to be identical in color, they were identical in every other way. And God, through His Spirit, is saying, "Recognize that you will have your own traits." Take advantage of this unique anointing. The Lord promises that there will be many various colors, but they will all connect to the same thing. And some of you are screaming, "When does this begin?" RIGHT NOW! Now is the time. According to the Lord, you will be fulfilled only if you fulfill the lofty call that I have set upon you. And when I say this, I'm not talking about a minor detail. You are the one I have picked. You've been drafted. It would be a crime to do anything else. Any other goal in life would be a heinous crime. My Spirit would appoint you as court marshals as a result of this. Are you up to the challenge? Yes, I am confident that you can. Keep in mind that the Dove is the head. You will be guided by the Spirit wherever you go. When you begin to lose heart, the Spirit will guide you to the ship of rest, which is a very natural thing to do. I'm not referring to the fact that we will simply rest. According to God, there will be natural boats for relaxation and healing. Some of them will be as large as Carnival Cruise Lines, but they will be dedicated solely to Eagles. According to God, there were as many ships as there were people who discovered America. In the world of the Spirits, numerous ships will reach unprecedented heights. The Spirits, the seven Spirits of God, I said. The Lord says, "I'm going to start using you." And it'll appear as if I've beaten you up. But the Lord says you're prepared and capable. I didn't pick the weak. I think I went with the bashful. It's possible that I went with the shy option. I think I went with the tense, jittery option. It's possible that I choose the ones that say I'll never do. The Lord, on the other hand, says NO means ON. And I'll put you on this plan that I've devised. And whether you realize it or not, this number has power. It's possible that one day there will be 12 eagles flying. The next day, it may be several hundred. It will be several thousand the next day. Part of the promise being realized has been the shifting and changing that has occurred in recent years. When I chose Judas, I knew he would betray me. As a result, what has been done is in the past. I had a good idea who would be available today. I knew just who I could utilize in this situation. I knew exactly who would be willing to carry out my instructions. Do you consider yourself to be kings? It's past time for you to wake up. You will see your reflections, eagles. It's important to remember that when these Eagles are in flight, they may have a leader. However, there is a true leader: the Holy Spirit. So, when you're flying, you're operating like a well-oiled machine, complete with all working and moving parts. When one of the Eagles is out of sync, the entire scheme is thrown off. And once these Eagles take to the air, their lives are no longer normal. No one knows about the Green Berets' private lives. When the FBI and CIA return home, they are unable to reveal anything about what they have in the military or the federal government. In heaven, these Eagles will reach an agreement in which secrets will be revealed to them. And then I saw the Word of God emblazoned across the chests of Eagles all of a sudden. Some of you would argue that I don't have the fullness of the Word in me or that I don't have the fullness of the Word upon me. It will be branded upon you, according to the Lord. Because the words will be branded on you like a hot iron, a hot brand, you will know things you should not know. As I was releasing this in the room, I felt a little anxiety and trembling, a bit anxious, because it's a big duty. If I didn't think you were ready, I would not have picked. This applies to children as well. There are no tiny eagles in the area. There is no variation in shape or size. There is no other brand that compares. They don't make it into a children's apple pie version of the Bible. It is the true Word of God that has been engraved on their hearts. And the Lord adds, "Whether you realize it or not, I am preparing you." I'll get you ready! Warriors of majesty. I am preparing you. One of the last things I need to make sure I get in here is that I saw the Eagles' eyes in the head of the Dove. They were literally on fire, burning. I'm going to draw this picture in some way. But the eyes were flaming, and there was a flickering of flame in the eyes as they burned. They returned to their original color. And I noticed that as Eagles flew over, their eyes would suddenly roll over into the flames of God as they looked down on the earth in par- ticular locations. It's the all-consuming fire, according to God. God's fear is what it is. It is the Lord's authority in the eyes of the people. It's witnessing through the piercing of the soul and spirit's separation. It's God's supernaturally convicting fire. The refiner's fire is the name given to that fire. It's that fire that sets off the chain reaction. And the

Lord says that every Eagle must have these eyes, eyes of fire, since this is exactly what I require at this time. Because, says the Spirit of God, My word declares that My eyes will be like fire in the end. My eyes will shine through you, just as they do through My Eagles, says the Spirit of God. I will appear to a large number of people, and I will do so with healing in My wings. But, if you're supposed to be like Me, and I, the Lord, am supposed to be like you, shouldn't we be using the same imagery? I'm forming an army that will resemble Me. Some people appear eerie and strange when they go to this degree. Some have been labeled as oddballs. You haven't become strange yet till you fully embrace what I'm doing. Ummm. Let's take it to the next level. I saw dragons with flames streaming out of their mouths when the Eagles flew over particular locations, as seen by the Spirit. The Eagles were being attacked by creatures. I saw snakes. I saw a leviathan, a python, and a swarm of spirits attempting to attack and infiltrate the very Eagles. And all of a sudden, I saw the Eagles flying together, and a large number of enemy soldiers on the ground were attempting to pierce the Eagles, kill them, or take them down. As they approached particular places, there were assignments against them to try to overtake them. They had a good idea they were coming and would try to get in. As they flew above, the Eagles became transparent. I'm causing stealth Eagles, according to God. They'll be able to fly and blend in when necessary, and they won't be hurt. God adds that when these Eagles acquire the totality of this, it will be as though they are flowing in the strength, power, and anointing of Michael the Archangel. Warriors! Because it's all about the One, these are humility Eagles. The Holy Spirit is always the guide, the head Eagle who is always God with healing in His wings, which is why the Dove stays at the top. In other words, they are more concerned with Him than with themselves. The color is the only part of ourselves that will be in the Eagle. The rest is all about Him. The only part of you that is of that Eagle is your own small bit of character, nature, and uniqueness. He is a military property, just like a Green Beret. I want you to go to the Middle East, says the military. I'd like you to photograph so and so. They're all set! They don't second-guess themselves. They are unconcerned about it. They put everything else aside and leave. When I say go, these warriors will go. When I say take flight, they'll take off. When the time comes, they will annihilate my adversary. These Eagles with the gavel, whether you realize it or not, understand that there will be, much like the slaying of the false prophets. It will be as if they are slaughtering the enemy by sounding the alarm. These Eagles, according to the Lord, will be anointed beyond anointing and will flow in the Spirit and power of Elijah and Moses. It's the pinnacle anointing of My authority and might in this final, final, final huge bang. The Eagles will one day land in vast numbers near the White House in the United States. And I see them covering the White House with their wings. And this is at a time when America is giving up the majority of her power. The Eagles will begin to defend the White House's values. I'm not talking about some president's house or bowling alley, but God has said that the Eagles will protect everything this country stands for. And even when governments try to —- and I'm not talking about US governments here; I'm talking about governments from other countries —- try to usurp America's rights, the Eagles will continue to defend America's rights, even if the US government gives it up for financial gain. It will appear to be correct. It will appear to be appropriate. However, it is associated with the anti-Christ movement. And the Eagles will be the last day prophets, serving as a guardian, an apostle, and a defender of America's vital rights. And until the very last day, when Satan is sent to his pit, shackled and unable to do anything. My Eagles will keep the United States of America believing in red, white, and blue. It could simply be a sliver of it. For the Lord declares that, just as Israel's measure has diminished piece by piece, chunk by chunk over the previous 100 years, the United States will do the same, giving up this and that. But, according to the Lord, the very last, very last thing that will happen is that they will know that they know that they know they are in the land of the free. In the Eagles, I saw the Garden of Eden being restored at long last by the Spirit of God. And it's as if it's enclosed in a protective dome; in other words, the enemy can't get in, and vice is forbidden. Only God's friends are permitted to enter this location, which contains the tree of life and the river of God, and which God predicts will be raised up as the last of the last. I'm restoring My Eden for My Eagles, says God. We congratulate you. We congratulate you.

I want you to understand that the oil runs easily when the Eagles extend their wings and fly above the fields. There will be no Eagle with less anointing than another. There may be a different release, but there will be enough oil for everyone. These are the replica Eagles. These are duplication Eagles. These are Eagles created in my likeness. Are you prepared for what's about to happen? Yes, some of you would say. And, one again, am I asking if you're ready for this? Like in a movie, there will be a day. As though you're ready to save the world, you'll be putting on your boots, putting on your jacket, and walking out the door. This is the kind of fighter I'm cultivating in this hour. You won't have to be afraid of dying. You won't have to worry about bullets, swords, or knives. You will not be afraid of bombardment. I will be with you if you grasp the fullness of this. And I'll look after you. Is this something you get?

Some of you are probably taken aback by this. I had no idea it was going to happen. "Look," God said, and I saw the Eagle. Even as I was releasing more unfurled, continuous vision, it continued to unfold. I could see you, but I could also see the vision that was taking place right in front of your eyes. It's as if the view is transparent, yet I can still see you there, always flowing. And there's a reason why God wants to show an image. There's a good explanation behind this. We must comprehend. Because every Eagle had the horn, this is a critical hour, a very critical hour. The gavel belonged to every Eagle. The passion in the eyes of every Eagle was palpable. The phrases were emblazoned on the chests of every Eagle. The anointing was on every Eagle. Every Eagle has a huge wing span and could fly for kilometers.

There are several details in this that some of you may have missed. Keep pressing into it until you get the full picture. Some of you might wish to jot down each little detail and try to imagine how God would elaborate on each one. This isn't something to be taken lightly. Some folks appear to be unconcerned about it. Don't take it lightly; it's the kind of thing where if you take it lightly, you'll tumble. This is a class project. You've been assigned to the role of special warriors. You've been assigned to be powerful warriors. You weren't chosen because you were inept. You were chosen because you have the ability to be exceptional. This isn't something you sign up for. This is something for which you were drafted. Accept what God has to say. You have nothing to be concerned about. Now and forever, praise God! All for the sake of Your Glory, Lord!

Milton Keynes UK
Ingram Content Group UK Ltd.
UKHW010133240823
427393UK00003B/43